THE

GREAT

STAYS

OF TEXAS

The Official Guide
to
Texas' Finest
Bed & Breakfasts,
Country Inns,
Hotels,
and
Guest Houses

... inspected and approved by
HISTORIC ACCOMMODATIONS
OF TEXAS (HAT)

Edited by: Sharry Buckner

THE GREAT STAYS OF TEXAS

Second Edition

Copyright © 1998

by Historic Accommodations of Texas, Inc.

Historic Accommodations of Texas, Inc. (HAT)
P.O. Box 1399, Fredericksburg, Texas 78624 (USA)

ISBN 0-9654752-1-2
Manufactured in the United States of America
Project Managed by HAT Guidebook Committee
Peter Delforge/The Delforge Place/Chairman
Production by Ocean-graphics
Cover design by Breez Studio
Printed by Visual Dimensions

Second Edition/First Printing
Library of Congress Catalog Card Number: 97-78284

Preface

"How did I get to be a hundred years old? Well, when I moves,
I moves slow. When I sits, I sits loose. And when I worries,
I goes to sleep."

--attributed to an old
Appalachian mountain woman

Welcome to the culmination of a long-standing dream. This book represents years of work by members of Historic Accommodations of Texas (HAT), who have set out to showcase Texas history in a way anyone can feel and embrace: by experiencing it overnight.

The members of our professional organization realize that today's travelers are increasingly sophisticated. While embracing the ambiance of days gone by, the traveling public also expects modern conveniences and standards. As a result, HAT adopted a strict set of guidelines which properties must meet in order to be members of our organization — and now, to appear in this book. This allows us to ensure that when you choose a HAT property, you'll not only find Texas history and Texas flavor, but Texas hospitality, cleanliness, comfort, and beauty.

The properties in this book range from pioneer homes and native stone cottages to glorious Victorian mansions and majestic city hotels. Each building played a part in shaping the rich and varied history of our state.

With over 800 inns in Texas, you have a lot of choices where to spend your leisure time. This book will help you make choices you will treasure.

We hope you'll try all the HAT lodgings featured in this guide. With the HAT logo as your "inn-surance", set out on your own Texas History Adventure! And while you're traveling, look for additional properties not presently listed. We're a dynamic, growing organization, and we're welcoming new members regularly.

We look forward to your visit!

Your hosts,

The members of
**HISTORIC ACCOMMODATIONS
OF TEXAS**

Why HAT Properties Are Different

Historic Accommodations of Texas (HAT) is an association of Texas' finest bed & breakfasts, country inns, hotels and guest houses, each with significant ties to Texas history. With members throughout the state, HAT is the traveling public's assurance that the accommodations selected measure up to high expectations.

To display the prized HAT logo, properties must be recognized historic buildings that are impeccably maintained and professionally managed. Members must also participate in regular inspection visits and educational programs.

Incorporating many of the stringent requirements set forth by AAA and Mobil, HAT's standards and guidelines have been customized to deal with structures of historical significance and requirements specific to the state of Texas. The result is a comprehensive inspection program which ensures a professional approach to all aspects of innkeeping, including demonstrated excellence in the following areas:

Historic Authenticity & Texas Flavor — restoration and preservation recognized by a national, state, or local historical society. For multiple-building complexes, at least one must carry historic designation and be accessible to guests.

Texas Hospitality & Professional Innkeeping — friendly, helpful, well-trained innkeepers and staff, as well as readily available tourist information.

Attractive Setting — well-maintained landscaping, courtyards, gardens, pools or hot tubs, with sufficient parking and exterior lighting.

Exemplary Housekeeping — impeccable cleanliness and interior upkeep, properly maintained heating, air conditioning and plumbing, and regular pest control.

Comfortable, Quality Furnishings — firm mattresses, quality bed and bath linens, bedside reading lights, ample space for guest movement, storage surfaces, and good lighting and ventilation.

Safety & Security — keyed deadbolt and privacy locks, precaution signs clearly posted, smoke detectors, safety outlets, fire extinguishers, and first aid kits.

Breakfast and/or Food Service That Strives For Excellence — an attractively-served breakfast using good quality dishes, glassware, and flatware at B&Bs and Inns; a restaurant or other food services at Hotels; a safe, sanitary kitchen environment at all properties.

How To Contact HAT:

For more information about HAT properties, membership materials, inspection criteria, or to comment on your stay at a featured property, please contact the organization at:

Historic Accommodations of Texas (HAT)
P.O. Box 1399 • Fredericksburg, Texas 78624
1-800-HAT-0368   www.hat.org

How To Use This Guidebook

ACCOMMODATION TYPES

With a wide variety of accommodations available today, choosing the one that is right for you can be confusing. To assist you, this guidebook uses four simple lodging categories:

Guest Houses — unhosted accommodations with either a continental or continental plus breakfast included. These are excellent choices for complete privacy, since travelers have the use of an entire house. In some cases, the property owner lives nearby; otherwise, the property is managed through a reservation agency. Guest houses are identified on the descriptive pages in the "BEDS" line.

Bed & Breakfasts — hosted properties that include breakfast in their room rate. Breakfast may range from simple, familiar selections to gourmet specialties. The host is usually a knowledgeable source of information on the community, local sightseeing, events, and restaurants.

Inns — the terms "inn" and "country inn" are often used interchangeably — not to imply these properties are found only in the country, but to give a sense of their ambiance. As such, inns are closer in definition to bed & breakfasts than to hotels. Generally, they tend to be larger than bed & breakfasts and may offer additional meal options or a high quality restaurant on the premises, yet still manage to retain the charm of an individual home.

Hotels — usually larger, multilevel commercial properties known for their wide range of guest services, rooms in several price categories, and on-premise food service. HAT membership also includes a growing number of small, intimate luxury or "boutique" hotels with outstanding personalized service and fine restaurants.

BREAKFASTS

Continental — coffee, tea, and one or more pastry options; some include juice

Continental Plus — an expanded continental menu of coffee, tea, pastries, juice and/or fresh fruit, and in some cases, a simple entree

Full Breakfast — a complete meal with hot entree, side dishes, juice and/or fresh fruit, and coffee or tea

Special Dietary Requirements — Most HAT properties accommodate special requests stemming from dietary concerns or food allergies. Please inquire when making reservations about a property's capabilities in this area. Advance notice is commonly required to arrange for dietary substitutions.

UNDERSTANDING THE SYMBOLS USED ON EACH PAGE

Symbols found on property page listings depict room rates, policies, and services. The guide below describes each symbol's intended meaning:

Room Rates: Dollar symbols reflect a property's published, per night price range for double occupancy. Additional persons in a room will result in extra charges, and state and local taxes will be added to the total bill. NOTE: rate ranges were accurate at press time, but are subject to change.

$ under $75 per night

$$ $75 - $100 per night

$$$ over $100 per night

Discounts & special rates — many properties offer reduced rates for weekday or off-season travel, extended stays, large groups, weddings and receptions, family reunions, or business travel. Please inquire when making reservations for individual property policies.

CC **Major Credit Cards Accepted:** Most properties accept some combination of VISA, MasterCard, American Express, Discover Card, Diners Club, or Carte Blanche. Properties not taking credit cards accept personal checks, cash and/or Travelers Checks. Gift certificates are available at most properties.

Children Allowed: Properties that accept children have their own policies as to the minimum age allowed. Many accept school age children and above. Few allow infants and toddlers. Remember that historic properties are hesitant to allow children due to the presence of fine antiques, valuable historical artifacts, or family heirlooms throughout the property. Please inquire when making reservations about each property's specific policy.

Pets Welcome: Guests traveling with pets will find their overnight options limited, but many hosts will help arrange overnight accommodations for pets at local facilities.

Smoking Allowed Inside: Only those properties which allow smoking inside (in guest-accessible areas) display this symbol on their page. However, most properties allow smoking outside in designated areas. Historic properties, as a rule, are stricter about this policy due to the age of the structure itself, the building materials used, or the presence of antiques.

Physically Challenged Accessibility: Properties which display this symbol offer some form of assistance for the physically challenged. This does not necessarily mean wheelchair accessibility, but may mean an aid such as bathroom handrails, walkway ramps, or equipment for the hearing impaired. Guests should consult with property owners to determine if their specific needs can be met.

THE GREAT STAYS OF TEXAS
Table of Contents

Preface 3

Why HAT Properties Are Different 4

How To Use This Guidebook 5

Table of Contents 7

HAT Properties In Texas (Map) 9

- *Abilene* 10
- *Austin* 11
- *Bay City* 15
- *Boerne* 16
- *Brenham* 18
- *Bryan* 21
- *Cleburne* 22
- *Columbus* 23
- *Comfort* 24
- *Conroe* 25
- *Crockett* 26
- *Dallas* 27
- *Del Rio* 28
- *Fort Davis* 30
- *Fort Worth* 31
- *Fredericksburg* 33
- *Glen Rose* 47
- *Gonzales* 48
- *Granbury* 50
- *Gruene* 53
- *Houston* 55

- *Huntsville* 56
- *Jefferson* 57
- *Kemah* 59
- *Luckenbach* 60
- *Marathon* 61
- *Martindale* 63
- *Mineola* 64
- *Navasota* 66
- *New Braunfels* 67
- *Palacios* 71
- *Pittsburg* 72
- *Rockport* 73
- *Round Top* 74
- *Salado* 76
- *San Antonio* 78
- *San Marcos* 85
- *Seabrook* 86
- *Seguin* 87
- *Smithville* 88
- *Spring* 89
- *Stephenville* 90
- *Tyler* 91
- *Vanderpool* 94
- *Waxahachie* 95
- *Winnsboro* 99

Famous and Favorite HAT Innkeepers' Recipes 101

Index of HAT Properties 124

Travel Log/Travel Notes 127

HAT Properties in Texas

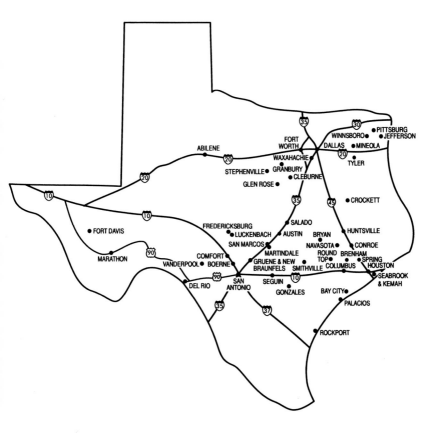

Historic Accommodations of Texas (HAT)
member properties can be found in all of the cities
identified on the above map.

Or, to get the most recent updates on all HAT member
property details - rooms, rates, phone numbers, websites
etc. - see our on-line guide at:

www.hat.org

Bolin's Prairie House

508 Mulberry
Abilene, TX 79601

800-673-5855
915-675-5855

Hosts: Sam and
Ginny Bolin

BEDS: 4 rooms, 2 private baths, 1 shared bath

BREAKFAST & OTHER MEALS: Full breakfast

$ Open all year

Bolin's Prairie House is charming and comfortable, blending antiques and modern luxuries to create a home-like atmosphere in the heart of Abilene. Built in 1902, the house was completely remodeled in 1920, obliterating all evidence of Victorian architecture in favor of the Frank Lloyd Wright Prairie style. In 1990, Sam and Ginny renovated it yet again to convert it to an attractive Bed & Breakfast. The downstairs common areas feature high ceilings, gleaming hardwood floors, and antique furnishings. Upstairs, the guest rooms are named Love, Joy, Peace, and Patience and are decorated to create similar moods. Ginny serves a luscious breakfast in the dining room, which features an extensive collection of cobalt depression glass and blue and white china.

Historical Significance:

Now an Abilene Historic Landmark, the home was purchased in 1904 by prominent businessman, Colonel Christmas Comfort Compere, as a family home.

Places To Go, Sites To See:

Abilene has an abundance of history. The tourist information bureau occupies the restored downtown railroad depot, the Paramount Theater is listed in the National Register of Historic Places, and the Grace Hotel (circa 1909) has been renovated to house three excellent museums. A short drive leads to Buffalo Gap Historic Village and Fort Phantom Hill.

Fairview -
A Bed and Breakfast Establishment

1304 Newning Ave.
Austin, TX 78704

800-310-4746
512-444-4746
Fax: 512-444-3494
E-Mail: fairview@io.com
Website:
www.fairview-bnb.com

Hosts: Duke and Nancy
       Waggoner

BEDS: 3 rooms, 3 suites, 6 private baths

BREAKFAST & OTHER MEALS: Full breakfast

$$, $$$ Open all year, two night minimum on selected weekends

Surrounded by enormous live oak trees, this turn-of-the-century Texas Colonial Revival style home offers gracious accommodations. Furnished with carefully selected antiques, the home is a tribute to the elegance of a bygone era. The luxurious, oversized guest rooms, located on the second floor, have private baths; some include screened-in porches or sunrooms. A guest kitchen provides a refrigerator and microwave. Two suites are offered in the Carriage House, each with private entrance, sitting room, full kitchen, eating area, bedroom, and bath. Guests gather in the Great Room and adjoining parlor overlooking the rose gardens. Lavishly landscaped gardens offer a peaceful retreat to enjoy complimentary refreshments and unwind after a busy day of activities.

Historical Significance:

Fairview, built about 1910, is an excellent example of Texas Colonial Revival style architecture. An early owner was Thomas A. Gullett. The house is designated an Austin Historic Landmark and received the 1993 Austin Heritage Society award for preservation of a historic building.

Places To Go, Sites To See:

Centrally located, Fairview is within minutes of I-35, the airport, all the attractions of downtown Austin, and has easy access to lakes in the Hill Country.

The Governors' Inn

611 West 22nd Street
Austin, TX 78705

800-871-8908
512-479-0638
Fax: 512-476-4769
E-Mail:
governorsinn@earthlink.net

Hosts: Lisa and Ed Mugford

BEDS: 10 rooms, 10 private baths

BREAKFAST & OTHER MEALS: Full breakfast; picnic lunches available with advance notice

$, $$, $$$ Open all year

Built in 1897, this neo-classical Victorian mansion was restored and christened The Governors' Inn in 1993. Each guest room is named for a governor from Texas' colorful past. The Inn is furnished with beautiful antiques, always with guests' comfort in mind. All rooms have private baths, individual telephone lines, and cable television. The Inn allows you to step back into Victorian elegance but provides all the modern necessities important to the discriminating traveler. Your hosts live off-site, but will ensure that guests are served a healthy breakfast each morning. The Governors' Inn is known for its delicious homemade Granola and sensitivity to those on an alternative diet. In addition to breakfast, fruit, non-fat yogurt and lower calorie items are always available. The hosts are happy to accommodate those with special dietary restrictions or allergies.

Historical Significance:

Captain Martin Kenney was the original owner of The Governors' Inn. He served in the Civil War, earning his rank in the Texas Cavalry Brigade. He later founded the Texas Historical Society.

Places To Go, Sites To See:

Located two blocks from the University of Texas campus, this B&B is convenient to the State Capitol and downtown Austin.

The McCallum House

613 W. 32nd Street
Austin, TX 78705

512-451-6744
Fax: 512-451-4752
E-mail:
McCallum@AustinTX.net

Hosts: Nancy and Roger Danley

BEDS: 3 rooms, 2 suites, 5 private baths

BREAKFAST & OTHER MEALS: Full breakfast

$$, $$$ Open all year, two night minimum on most weekends, three night minimum on holiday weekends

The McCallum House, Austin's first Bed & Breakfast, opened in 1983 and is rated excellent by AAA and Mobil. All luxurious suites and rooms have private baths, private porches, and private kitchen facilities; two have private entrances. In addition, Nancy and Roger have thoughtfully provided, in each guest room, such "extras" as cable television, private phone with answering machine, built-in hair dryer, iron and ironing board, and sitting/work areas. One suite has a whirlpool tub, another has 12½-foot ceilings and a sky-lighted bathroom. Guests may enjoy breakfast served in the formal dining room or may choose a breakfast tray delivered to their room.

Historical Significance:

Built in 1907 for A. N. and Jane Y. McCallum, the house is listed in the National Register of Historic Places, a Recorded Texas Historic Landmark, an Austin Landmark, and recipient of a Heritage Society award. Jane Y. McCallum was a leader in the woman's suffrage movement and later directed the famous "Petticoat Lobby." She was Secretary of State for both governors Dan Moody and Ross Sterling. During her first term, she found an original copy of the Texas Declaration of Independence.

Places To Go, Sites To See:

The McCallum House is just north of the University of Texas campus and conveniently located to Austin's unlimited choices of activities.

Woodburn House

4401 Avenue D
Austin, TX 78751-3714

512-458-4335
Fax: 512-458-4319
E-mail:
woodburn@iamerica.net
Website:
www.woodburnhouse.com

Hosts: Sandra and Herb
Dickson

BEDS: 4 rooms, 4 private baths

BREAKFAST & OTHER MEALS: Full breakfast

Open all year, two night minimum on most holidays and special events weekends

Woodburn House sits on a large corner lot in Hyde Park, a National Register historic neighborhood of enormous old trees and quiet streets, creating a sense of rural tranquility. Built in 1909, the home is furnished with period American antiques, some of which have been in the Dickson family since before the turn of the century. Herb and Sandra invite guests to enjoy the comforts of their home. Each of the four spacious guest rooms has its own character, a comfortable rocking chair, desk and phone, private bath, firm mattress and luxurious linens on queen or king-size beds. Enjoy morning breezes or tranquil afternoons on the wraparound porches. A gourmet breakfast, planned to meet guests' dietary requirements, is served. The "Austin Chronicle" selected the Woodburn House as the "Best Bed & Breakfast in Austin" for 1996.

Historical Significance:

This 1909 Austin Landmark was moved from its original lot to protect it from demolition. Woodburn House is the only remaining original Hyde Park residence with wraparound porches on both levels. It is considered a contributing member of the National Register Historic District.

Places To Go, Sites To See:

Woodburn House is minutes from the municipal airport, all the attractions of downtown Austin, the University of Texas campus, several fine restaurants, and within walking distance of a park with pool and tennis courts.

Bailey House

1704 Third Street
Bay City, TX 77414

409-245-5613
Fax: 409-244-8479

Host: Sue Bailey

BEDS: 3 rooms, 1 private bath, 1 shared bath

BREAKFAST & OTHER MEALS: Continental Plus breakfast

$$ Open all year

This stately, turn-of-the-century Classical Revival home features spacious rooms with period furniture and oriental carpets. Sue and her husband have traveled extensively and collected mementos and furnishings from around the world. Beautiful quilts are displayed, which is no surprise since Sue owns a quilt shop in Bay City and teaches classes. Guest accommodations are upstairs. Verandas stretch across the back, both upstairs and down, overlooking the butterfly garden in the shade of magnolia trees. Breakfast is served in the formal dining room.

Historical Significance:

A Recorded Texas Historic Landmark built in 1910 by the Kilbride family, this gracious home remained in the family for over eight decades. It was the site of many early Bay City social functions.

Places To Go, Sites To See:

Nearby attractions include the historic town square of Bay City with "Market Days" every third Saturday, an 18-hole Gary Player-designed golf course, and bird-watching along the great South Texas Birding Trail.

Guadalupe River Ranch

605 FM 474
Boerne, TX 78006

800-460-2005
830-537-4837
E-Mail:
grranch@connecti.com

Host: Elisa McClure

BEDS: 43 rooms, 3 suites, 42 private baths, 3 shared baths

BREAKFAST & OTHER MEALS: Full breakfast; lunch and dinner with advance reservations

$$$ Open all year except December 20-26, 1998

The main lodge, built in 1929, has been restored to its original rustic grandeur. Accommodations vary from charming stone cottages nestled among oak trees to bluffside rooms with private balconies and majestic views of the river and distant hills. Three are two-bedroom suites; all are comfortably furnished. The 360-acre ranch can accommodate up to 100 and is an ideal place for romance, reunions and retreats. Its sprawling, landscaped grounds retain the feel of a magnificent estate. Credit goes to Mother Nature for providing one of the most spectacular views in the Texas Hill Country and to the staff at Guadalupe River Ranch for providing excellent service and renowned gourmet cuisine.

Historical Significance:

In 1929, the president of Alamo National Bank, Walter Napier, built the main lodge and later sold it to actress Olivia de Havilland. A grotto, now used as a tiny chapel, dates to the 1800s.

Places To Go, Sites To See:

Guadalupe River Ranch provides first class recreational and fitness facilities, including exercise equipment, game room with pool table and ping pong, tennis court, swimming pool, sauna and hot tub. Nature provides unspoiled acreage for horseback riding and hiking, scenic trails for adventuring, and miles of the Guadalupe River for tubing and canoeing.

Ye Kendall Inn

128 W. Blanco
Boerne, TX 78006

800-364-2138
830-249-2138

Hosts: Shane and Vicki Schleyer

BEDS: 9 rooms, 4 suites, 13 private baths

BREAKFAST & OTHER MEALS: Continental Plus breakfast; restaurant & Tea Room on premises

$$, $$$ Open all year, two night minimum on holiday weekends

Ye Kendall Inn is a two-story hotel featuring 20-inch-thick native stone walls. Shane and Vicki's extensive restoration has brought back the beauty of the hardwood floors, original front desk, fireplaces, and 200-foot front porch with railings and columns. All guest rooms are decorated with period antiques and most have queen-size beds; all include private baths, some with antique claw foot tubs. The main floor of the inn contains the parlor where breakfast is served, an Italian restaurant, and a boutique. The courtyard leads to the Antique Shopping Village made up of relocated and restored structures and historic buildings. Five acres of grounds extend down to Cibolo Creek.

Historical Significance:

Ye Kendall Inn is a Recorded Texas Historic Landmark and is listed in the National Register of Historic Places. It was originally built in 1859 as a residence for Erastus and Sarah Reed, who brought the Southern Colonial style of architecture to the Texas Hill Country. The wings were added in 1878; it opened as The Boerne Hotel and served as a stagecoach inn throughout the 1880s.

Places To Go, Sites To See:

The German influence of original settlers is still apparent in the architecture of Boerne's historic downtown district. There's something for everyone – shopping, sightseeing, family activities, and year-round local events.

Ant Street Inn

107 West Commerce
Brenham, TX 77833

800-481-1951
409-836-7393
Fax: 409-836-7595
E-Mail: stay@antstreetinn.com
Website: www.antstreetinn.com

Hosts: Pam and Tommy Traylor

BEDS: 13 rooms, 13 private baths

BREAKFAST & OTHER MEALS: Full breakfast; meals for business meetings
or group events available with prior arrangements

$$, $$$ Open all year

This turn-of-the-century inn combines the finest in Deep South hospitality,
warmth, and elegance with the convenience and personal service of a first class
hotel. Pam and Tommy have furnished the Inn with an outstanding collection of
American antiques, including exceptionally exquisite beds. The guest rooms
feature twelve-foot ceilings, polished hardwood floors with Oriental rugs,
telephones, cable televisions, and individual climate controls. Some have sitting
areas, desks, stained-glass windows, or tubs for two. The rocking chairs on the
back balcony overlooking the courtyard invite relaxation. Whether it's business
or pleasure that brings you to Brenham, the Ant Street Inn offers a nineteenth-
century retreat for the twentieth-century traveler.

Historical Significance:

The Schmid brothers, Swiss immigrants, built this two-story brick Renaissance
Revival building in 1899 for their thriving mercantile business. Throughout the
next ninety years, the building housed a grocery store, feed store, café, gambling
hall, wrestling matches, and finally a bed and breakfast inn.

Places To Go, Sites To See:

There are many shops, restaurants, and nightspots in the adjacent Ant Street area.
The rolling hills of Washington County offer attractions such as Blue Bell
Creameries, The Antique Rose Emporium, the Monastery of St. Clare, and local
museums.

Far View - A Bed & Breakfast Inn

1804 S. Park Street
Brenham, TX 77833

888-FAR-VIEW
409-836-1672
Fax: 409-836-5893
E-mail:
farview@phoenix.net
Website:
www.bbhost.com/farview

Hosts: David and Tonya Meyer

BEDS: 5 rooms, 5 private baths

BREAKFAST & OTHER MEALS: Full breakfast

$$, $$$ Open all year

Experience Great Gatsby-era elegance in a completely renovated 1925 home listed as a Recorded Texas Historic Landmark. Its location on a hill with a distant view of unsurpassed beauty was the inspiration for its name, Far View. The Inn has been lovingly restored and decorated by David and Tonya. Guest rooms are comfortably furnished and include queen or king-size beds, individual thermostats, and telephones. Data ports are available for business travelers. Surrounding Far View, two acres of landscaped gardens, 70-year-old live oaks, and grassy expanses of lawn set the scene for a lazy game of croquet. Guests also enjoy spending time by the swimming pool. An abundant gourmet breakfast is served at the 1930s Chippendale dining room suite, with sun streaming through six stained glass windows.

Historical Significance:

In 1924, physician Dr. Walter F. Hasskarl purchased acreage on a hill with a magnificent view of the surrounding countryside and hired Houston architect Alfred C. Finn, whose works include the San Jacinto Monument, to design a home befitting the site. Dr. Hasskarl played an integral part in the success of Brenham, providing health care and promoting civic activities.

Places To Go, Sites To See:

Attractions and activities in the Brenham area are many and varied. Washington-on-the-Brazos, birthplace of the Republic of Texas, is well worth a visit.

Mariposa Ranch

8904 Mariposa Lane
Brenham, TX 77833

409-836-4737
Fax: 409-836-4737

Hosts: Johnna and Charles
Chamberlain

BEDS: 9 rooms, 7 private baths, 2 shared baths

BREAKFAST & OTHER MEALS: Full breakfast; Meals for group events

$$, $$$ Open all year, two night minimum on special events weekends

Mariposa Ranch has a special spirit all its own, traveling back 165 years. A variety of accommodations are available in five separate buildings, all lovingly restored and furnished with period antiques. The main house, an 1870 Plantation home, offers two spacious rooms with 12-foot ceilings and queen-size beds. The 1825 Texas Ranger Log Cabin features a huge stone fireplace and upstairs sleeping loft. Two luxurious suites, each with two fireplaces, comprise the Independence House, built in 1836. Fern Oaks Cottage is cozy with a fireplace and queen-size bed, and the Reinauer Guest House is a completely restored turn-of-the-century Texas farmhouse with three bedrooms. The Chamberlains offer special "Enchanted Evening" romance packages and massages. Mariposa (Spanish for butterfly) Ranch is a place with an excellent blend of pampering and privacy.

Historical Significance:

Four of the five buildings are historical, dating back as far as 1825. The Reinauer Guest House is the original homestead. Mariposa Ranch has been featured in *Texas Highways, Southern Living,* and *Country Inns* magazines, and has been on several Washington County Historical Society tours.

Places To Go, Sites To See:

Mariposa Ranch is on the famous LaBahia Road, the first historical highway named in Texas. It is located near numerous Washington County attractions and spectacular fields of bluebonnets in the spring.

Angelsgate Bed & Breakfast

615 East 29th Street
Bryan, TX 77803

888-779-1231
or 409-779-1231
Fax: 409-822-6131
E-Mail: angels@txcyber.com
Website: www2.cy-net.net/~angels

Hosts: Gary and Beth Goyen

BEDS: 4 suites, 4 private baths

BREAKFAST & OTHER MEALS: Full breakfast; dinner available with prior arrangements

$$ Open all year

Stepping through the leaded-glass entry of Angelsgate is like a passage through time to a day when entertaining visitors was a grand event. Richly restored with 11-foot ceilings, stained-glass windows, dark polished woods, and gleaming chandeliers, this outstanding home is furnished with American and French antiques. Guests may choose from two elegant upstairs suites, the Carriage House, or the Cottage next door. Each suite is equipped with cable television, video player, telephone, and data port. Restore your spirits amid the flowers and lush greenery in the garden gazebo. Breakfast fare may be American country, Mexican migas, or French angel fruit toast, all worthy of both angels and guests at this special bed and breakfast.

Historical Significance:

The American Foursquare style reflects the architectural trend of the times toward simplicity of design. Built in 1909 for Allister M. Waldrop, Sr. and his wife, Nanne, both active civic leaders of the community, it was the family residence until 1978. Listed in the National Register of Historic Places in 1983, the home was designated a Recorded Texas Historic Landmark in 1987.

Places To Go, Sites To See:

Angelsgate is located in the heart of Bryan's Historical District, a five minute drive to the Texas A&M University campus, convenient to the George Bush Presidential Library, Messina Hof Winery, and walking distance to the Brazos County Courthouse and revitalized downtown area.

Cleburne's 1896 Railroad House B&B

421 E. Henderson Street
Cleburne, TX 76031

800-668-1896
817-517-5529
Fax: 817-517-5529

Host: Quilla Perkins

BEDS: 4 rooms, 2 private baths, 1 shared bath

BREAKFAST & OTHER MEALS: Full breakfast

$$ Open all year

Quilla opened Cleburne's 1896 Railroad House Bed & Breakfast in the summer of 1996, the one-hundredth birthday of the building. At the top of the stairs, guests enter the lobby and see the old Hotel Santa Fe, the high pressed tin ceilings, transom windows… and can almost hear a distant train whistle. This second floor hotel has been restored, but the ambiance has been maintained with railroad memorabilia displayed throughout. Guest room doors still have the original ivory numbers and brass sign plates. Today, the rooms have names such as The Locomotive, The Pullman, and the Caboose. Relax in the skylighted lobby, read or watch TV in the library.

Historical Significance:

Built as a Railroad Hotel in 1896 by the Poindexters, both from prominent Cleburne families, it was used by railroad workers and passengers during Cleburne's boom days. Part of the "Save Old Cleburne" historical preservation society, it is one of the few remaining railroad hotels currently in operation.

Places To Go, Sites To See:

Visit the Layland Museum, the 1912 Johnson County Courthouse, nearby Pat Cleburne State Park, Dinosaur Valley, Lake Whitney, or Fossil Rim Wildlife Park.

Magnolia Oaks Bed & Breakfast

634 Spring Street
Columbus, TX 78934

409-732-2726

Hosts: Bob and Nancy Stiles

BEDS: 5 rooms, 5 private baths

BREAKFAST & OTHER MEALS: Full breakfast

$$, $$$ Open all year, two night minimum during special events weekends

A Recorded Texas Historical Landmark, Magnolia Oaks is located two blocks west of the historic courthouse square in Columbus. Guests enter the 1890 Victorian from twin gingerbread porches. The spacious guest rooms are furnished with antiques and offer private baths (one with a Jacuzzi); two have fireplaces, one features a giant Texas cedar bed, another overlooks the summer room and has its own balcony. Amenities include fresh flowers, afternoon treats, special toiletries, robes, bikes, croquet, and a chipping green. The garden with its fountain inspires a feeling of quietude. Bob and his guitar offer a "Toast to the Morning" before the bountiful breakfast.

Historical Significance:

A Texas historical marker notes the site was first a railway hospital, which burned in 1886. This Eastlake mansion, built on the site in 1890, was the home of Texas Representative Marcus H. Townsend, later Senator Townsend.

Places To Go, Sites To See:

Columbus is on a bend in the Colorado River, an easy drive from Houston, Austin, and San Antonio. Enjoy a production at the restored historic Stafford Opera House, tour several local museums, see the nearby Painted Churches of Schulenburg, and browse through local antique and gift shops.

The Meyer B&B on Cypress Creek

845 High Street
Comfort, TX 78013

800-364-2138
830-995-2304
E-mail: shane@texas.net
www.io.com/~bjmeyer/hotel.html

Host: Shane Schleyer

BEDS: 9 rooms, 9 private baths

BREAKFAST & OTHER MEALS: Full breakfast

$, $$ Open all year, two night minimum on holidays and during special events

The Meyer Bed & Breakfast on Cypress Creek offers a peaceful, relaxing setting in the heart of the Texas Hill Country. The complex consists of six renovated buildings just one block from Comfort's quaint historic district. Each suite or unit offers a private bath, cable TV, air conditioning, and is furnished and decorated with a rustic country theme. Breakfast is served each morning in the large dining room overlooking Cypress Creek. A vine-covered gazebo and a sizable screened porch, complete with wood stove and game boards, also have scenic views of the creek. The accommodations and spacious grounds make this an ideal place for group gatherings, an escape from crowds, an opportunity to enjoy a slower pace.

Historical Significance:

As a Recorded Texas Historic Landmark property, the Meyer's buildings each have their own story to tell. The oldest, the Stage Stop Depot, was built in 1857 to serve as the last stagecoach stop before crossing the Guadalupe River going toward San Antonio. The newest is the Meyer Hotel built in 1920.

Places To Go, Sites To See:

Comfort, founded in 1854, boasts over one hundred pre-1900 buildings in its National Historic District, many located in what is considered Texas' most complete 19th-century business district. Many of these buildings house antique shops, gift boutiques, art galleries, and eateries. The "Treue Der Union" monument in Comfort is the only monument to the Union south of the Mason-Dixon line.

Heather's Glen...
A Bed & Breakfast and More!

200 East Phillips
Conroe, TX 77301

800-66-JAMIE
409-441-6611
Fax: 409-441-6603
E-Mail:
 heathersbb@aol.com

Hosts: Ed and Jamie George

BEDS: 5 rooms, 3 suites, 8 private baths

BREAKFAST & OTHER MEALS: Full breakfast

$, $$, $$$ Open all year, two night minimum on holidays and major events weekends

Ed and Jamie welcome guests to the former Wahrenberger turn-of-the-century Victorian mansion. After extensive restoration, Heather's Glen now entertains guests from all over the world. The mansion features 12-foot ceilings, gleaming heart-of-pine floors throughout, formal parlors and shaded verandas surrounding the home. Elegantly furnished with period antiques, the home offers a Victorian flair without sacrificing modern comforts. Across the street, Heather's Cottage offers three luxury suites, each with a private entrance, private bath with Jacuzzi, and furnished with European antiques. Grace and elegance are hallmarks of this beautiful inn.

Historical Significance:

This grand, two-story mansion was built at the turn of the century as the private residence for one of Conroe's wealthiest families. The home was used briefly as a boarding house for single school teachers as the Wahrenbergers had no children of their own.

Places To Go, Sites To See:

Nearby attractions include Old Town Spring and Old Town Montgomery, with antique and gift shops, art galleries, and restaurants. Heather's Glen is also convenient to Lake Conroe and the Victorian Southern Empress paddleboat, golf courses, swimming, theme parks, a large outlet mall and antique auctions.

Warfield House

712 East Houston Ave.
Crockett, TX 75835

888-988-8800
409-544-4037
E-Mail: jcostler@sat.net
Website: www.virtualcities.com/
ons/tx/z/txz4601.htm

Hosts: Judy and James Ostler

BEDS: 4 rooms, 4 private baths

BREAKFAST & OTHER MEALS: Full breakfast

$$ Open all year

The Warfield House, a completely restored 1897 stately Victorian home in historic Crockett, features modern conveniences while maintaining the elegant style and grace of a bygone era. Furnishings throughout the home consist of European and American period antiques including many family heirlooms. The formal parlor and dining room are used for entertaining and buffet breakfasts. An enclosed back porch, overlooking the outdoor pool and deck areas, offers a more informal setting. Guest rooms are upstairs and tastefully decorated with rich colors, attractive wallcoverings and window treatments to give each a unique personality. Your hostess is a Crockett native and very knowledgeable about the area and its history.

Historical Significance:

Among the oldest and finest homes in Crockett, The Warfield House is located on part of the El Camino Real, the oldest traveled route in Texas, and along Crockett's "silk stocking street" as it was known at the turn of the century. The Warfields were prominent citizens of the community, and their home boasted the town's first indoor plumbing and cistern.

Places To Go, Sites To See:

Named for frontiersman Davy Crockett, the town is the seat of Houston County, the first county formed in the Republic of Texas in 1837. Houston County has over 200 historical markers. The area offers numerous lakes for recreation, water sports, and fishing. Davy Crockett National Forest, Mission Tejas State Park, and Caddoan Indian Mounds State Park are nearby, and the vintage downtown "picture show" is only $1.50.

Hôtel St. Germain

2516 Maple Avenue
Dallas, TX 75201

214-871-2516

Host: Claire L. Heymann,
Proprietor

BEDS: 7 suites, 7 private baths

BREAKFAST & OTHER MEALS: Continental Plus breakfast; restaurant offers prix fixe ($75) five-course gourmet dinners Tuesday through Saturday with advance reservations.

$$$ Open all year except ten days in August and Christmas Day

This award-winning boutique hotel offers seven luxury suites, two parlors, two dining rooms, and a New Orleans-style courtyard as a tranquil oasis for travelers to a busy city. All suites are lavishly decorated with turn-of-the-century French antiques and feature elaborately canopied beds, fireplaces, and cable television. Guests will find Jacuzzis or soaking tubs, European toiletries, and signature terrycloth robes for lounging. Additionally, the conveniences of a 24-hour concierge, a butler, room service, valet parking and business services are available. Breakfast consists of cafe au lait, fresh fruit compote, and a sumptuous assortment of specialty breads and French pastries created by the hotel chef. The hotel is available for catering, banquets, weddings, and special events.

Historical Significance:

Built in 1909 as one of the first residences on Maple Avenue by prominent businessman John Patrick Murphy, this fashionable home was occupied by three generations of his family until the 1950s. Claire Heymann purchased the Victorian house in 1990 and began extensive renovations to create the splendid Hôtel St. Germain.

Place To Go, Sites To See:

The European-style Hôtel St. Germain is located adjacent to the shops and restaurants of The Crescent, the McKinney Avenue area, and the gallery district along Fairmount and Maple Avenues.

The 1890 House Bed & Breakfast Inn

609 Griner St.
Del Rio, TX 78840

800-282-1360
830-775-8061
Fax: 830-775-4667

Hosts: Laura and Alberto
Galvan

BEDS: 3 rooms, 2 suites, 5 private baths

BREAKFAST & OTHER MEALS: Full breakfast

$$, $$$ Open all year, two night minimum for holidays and special events

Alberto and Laura realized their dream when they found this magnificent historic home in the heart of downtown Del Rio, within walking distance of churches, shopping, and parks. Now they invite guests to enjoy the serenity of its verandas, private gardens, and numerous, ancient pecan trees. Five guest accommodations, each beautifully furnished with period antiques, feature king or queen-size four-poster beds, television, air conditioning, and private baths with Jacuzzi or oversized soaking tubs. Guests may curl up in front of the fireplace with a good book from the library, relax in the garden beside a crystal clear stream, or nap on the veranda. Make your visit an international event by traveling three miles for South of the Border shopping and dining in Acuna, Mexico.

Historical Significance:

Built circa 1890 by Del Rio's first doctor and presented as a gift to his wife, Belle Josephine Price-Woods, this home is currently listed in "A Guide To Historic Del Rio." Its architecture resembles the antebellum plantations of the south.

Places To Go, Sites To See:

Sites in the area include the Alamo Village movie location, Amistad Lake, the Roy Bean Historic Site, Whitehead Museum, Val Verde Winery, and archeological sites. Horseback riding, golf, water skiing, fishing, and tennis are nearby.

La Mansion Del Rio 1887

123 Hudson Drive
Del Rio, TX 78840

800-995-1887
830-768-1100

Hosts: Jay, Barbara, and
Elizabeth Johnson

BEDS: 4 rooms, 2 private baths, 1 shared bath

BREAKFAST & OTHER MEALS: Full breakfast

$$, $$$ Open all year, two or three night minimum during special events and holidays

Near the Mexican border, two acres of landscaped grounds with centurion pecan trees, magnolias, and palms surround La Mansion Del Rio. An impressive hacienda-style structure, the home retains many original features such as imported hand-painted Italian tiled floors, forged iron gates, archways, columns, and imported Mediterranean cypress beamed ceilings. Exquisite hand-painted murals adorn each window in the ballroom-sized living room. Guest accommodations are comfortable and beautifully appointed. One grand suite is on the first floor off the foyer, the other three are on the second floor. A wholesome breakfast is served in the formal dining room with its cathedral ceiling and century-old chandelier or in the shaded Mexican tiled courtyard.

Historical Significance:

A Recorded Texas Historic Landmark, this 4600-sq. ft. mansion was once the home of Judge John Foster. Built in 1887, it is one of the oldest mansions in the region and was the first to enjoy such modern conveniences as electricity and indoor plumbing.

Places To Go, Sites To See:

Attractions in Del Rio include the adjacent historical Val Verde Winery and the Whitehead Memorial Museum where Judge Roy Bean is buried. Nearby Lake Amistad offers water recreation and fishing. La Mansion Del Rio is only a few minutes' drive from the main shopping and dining areas of Acuna, Mexico.

The Hotel Limpia

On the Town Square
Fort Davis, TX 79734

800-662-5517
915-426-3237
Fax: 915-426-3983
Website:
www.hotellimpia.com

Hosts: Joe and Lanna Duncan

BEDS: 21 rooms, 14 suites, 1 cottage, 36 private baths

BREAKFAST & OTHER MEALS: None included; lunch and dinner available Tuesday - Sunday in the Hotel Limpia Dining Room

$, $$, $$$ Open all year

The Hotel Limpia is a restored historic hotel built in 1912, located in the heart of the Davis Mountains of southwest Texas. Guest accommodations are in the original hotel, three nearby restored historic buildings, a mountain cottage, and a Victorian adobe home. All feature period furnishings and decor. The 12-foot tin ceilings, upstairs walls with rounded corners, and much of the turn-of-the-century oak furniture remain today. An outstanding gift shop, nature store, bookstore, private club, and excellent dining room are adjacent. The courtyard garden, fragrant with roses and herbs, the enormous glassed-in veranda with its flourishing plants, and the porches with dozens of rocking chairs are favorite places for guests to relax and hide from the busy world.

Historical Significance:

Named for a nearby mountain creek, the original structure was constructed in 1912, using pink limestone quarried near Sleeping Lion Mountain. Through the years, the hotel served as the center of the ranching community. Today, the Hotel Limpia is much as it was when judges, doctors, and politicians came to Fort Davis to escape the sultry summers to the south and east.

Places To Go, Sites To See:

Visit the impressive McDonald Observatory which has special viewing programs for visitors. Explore Fort Davis National Historic Site and Big Bend National Park.

Miss Molly's Hotel

109 ½ W. Exchange Avenue
Fort Worth, TX 76106

800-99MOLLY
817-626-1522
Fax: 817-625-2723
E-Mail:
missmollys@travelbase.com
Website: www.missmollys.com

Hosts: Alice and Mark Hancock

BEDS: 8 rooms, 1 private bath, 3 shared baths

BREAKFAST & OTHER MEALS: Continental Plus breakfast

$$, $$$ Open all year except Thanksgiving and Christmas Days

Once a prim and proper boarding house, later a popular bordello, now a historic hotel operating in the true bed and breakfast tradition…Miss Molly's Hotel offers eight authentic turn-of-the-century boarding house rooms that surround a central parlor, lighted predominantly by a stained glass skylight. Seven of the rooms share three antique-appointed full bathrooms (robes are provided during your stay). The largest room, Miss Josie's, boasts fancy Victorian decor with a draped fabric ceiling and a private bath. The other rooms are reminiscent of hotel rooms in old western movies with names like The Gunslinger, Cattleman, Oilman, Railroader, and Cowboy.

Historical Significance:

Built in 1910, the second story of this commercial building opened as a straight-laced rooming house. By the mid-1940s, the area had succumbed to a rowdier lifestyle, and this floor became a bawdy house known as "The Gayette Hotel".

Places To Go, Sites To See:

The Stockyards National Historic District is a unique specialty dining, shopping, and entertainment area that includes Billy Bob's Texas, the Cowtown Coliseum, the station for the 100-year-old restored Tarantula Excursion Railroad, and a Museum in the Livestock Exchange Building.

The Texas White House

1417 Eighth Avenue
Fort Worth, TX 76104

800-279-6491
817-923-3597
Fax: 817-923-0410

E-Mail: txwhitehou@aol.com

Hosts: Jamie and Grover McMains

BEDS: 3 rooms, 3 private baths

BREAKFAST & OTHER MEALS: Full breakfast

$$$ Open all year

A City of Fort Worth Historic Landmark, this country-style home was awarded the Historic Preservation Council Pedestal Award for restoration to its original 1910 grandeur. Furnished with simple, yet elegant decor, the three upstairs guest rooms each have a queen-size bed with a choice of pillows and featherbeds on request, comfortable sitting area, and private bath with claw foot tub for soaking bubble baths or showers. Guests may enjoy the parlor, living room with fireplace, dining room, and large wrap-around porch, or be afforded complete privacy if desired. Special services may be arranged for business travelers. Breakfast may be served in either the dining room or to guest rooms and will be a gourmet treat with seasonal fresh fruit or baked fruit in compote, egg casseroles, homemade breads and muffins, juices, coffee and tea.

Historical Significance:

Known as the Bishop-Newkirk house, the structure is a classic example of a hipped cottage, an architecture later known as the Open Plan. It was the boyhood home of Richard C. Newkirk, former Mayor of Fort Worth and architect of the Fort Worth Cultural District. The house was the Newkirk family home for 49 years in one of the original exclusive neighborhoods in Fort Worth.

Places To Go, Sites To See:

Located on the edge of the medical district of Fort Worth, the Texas White House is just minutes from downtown, Sundance Square, the Fort Worth Zoo, Texas Christian University, the Botanic Gardens, the historic Stockyards, and the Cultural District.

Austin Street Retreat

Gästehaus Schmidt Reservation Service
231 W. Main
Fredericksburg, TX 78624

830-997-5612
E-Mail: gasthaus@ktc.com
Website: see bottom of page
Owners: Cynthia England and
David Clements

BEDS: Guest Houses - 5 suites, 5 private baths

BREAKFAST & OTHER MEALS: Continental breakfast

$$, $$$ Open all year, two night minimum on holiday and special event weekends

The Austin Street Retreat is an unusual compound of individual stone cottage suites, courtyards, and fountains. The original family home, circa 1867, manifests the German pioneer building techniques that make Fredericksburg's architecture so distinctive and enduring. The owner has an eye for premium quality furnishings and amenities and has made this a most appealing retreat. Each suite is individually appointed and totally different, but has a queen or king-size bed, whirlpool tub for two, phone, central heat and air, and coffee bar with microwave, refrigerator, and sink. Continental breakfasts are provided in the kitchen areas of these unhosted suites.

Historical Significance:

Located in Fredericksburg's National Historic District, this limestone, log, and stucco compound began as a family home for German immigrants. Lovingly and artistically restored in 1976, the property has been expanded and includes fountains surrounded by vine-covered walls, the original windmill, and a wealth of historic beauty.

Places To Go, Sites To See:

Visit Enchanted Rock State Park, take drives in the scenic countryside famous for its spring wildflowers, explore the many restaurants and shops.

Websites:

www.ktc.net/GSchmidt/annies.htm
www.ktc.net/GSchmidt/eljefe.htm
www.ktc.net/GSchmidt/asmaria.htm

www.ktc.net/GSchmidt/asreli.htm
www.ktc.net/GSchmidt/kristin.htm

Country Cottage Inn

405 E. Main
249 E. Main (Office)
Fredericksburg, TX 78624

830-997-8549

Host: Mary Lou Rodriquez,
Mgr.

BEDS: 2 rooms, 2 suites, 4 private baths

BREAKFAST & OTHER MEALS: Full breakfast

$$, $$$, Open all year, no restrictions

This beautifully preserved home was built in 1850 by Frederick Kiehne, a blacksmith and cutler by trade. The first two-story limestone house in Fredericksburg, it is constructed of native two-foot thick limestone walls, hand-cut beams and woodwork; the original stone fireplace is still functional today. Handmade arched doors lead from the porch to cool whitewashed stone rooms. Exposed rafters are hand cut from solid post oak heartwood. The guest rooms are tastefully furnished in antiques, many locally made in Fredericksburg in the mid 1800s. Each features a king or queen-size bed, room refrigerator, coffee maker, television, and telephone. Two of the private baths have large Jacuzzi tubs. Romance, relaxation, and comfort are top priorities at Country Cottage Inn.

Historical Significance:

Listed in the National Register of Historic Places, Fredericksburg's first stone house is a Recorded Texas Historic Landmark. It was built around 1850 by Frederick Kiehne who sailed from Hanover, Germany with his wife, Maria. Their names are inscribed on the keystone over the front door.

Places To Go, Sites To See:

The Nimitz Museum is just across the street and the Nimitz birthplace is in the next block. Step out the door and find more history, as well as antique and gift shops and many fine restaurants which line both sides of Main Street.

Das College Haus

106 W. College Street
Fredericksburg, TX 78624

800-654-2802
830-997-9047
E-mail: myrna@hctc.net

Host: Myrna Dennis
and Tim Saska

BEDS: 4 rooms, 4 private baths

BREAKFAST & OTHER MEALS: Full breakfast

$$, $$$ Open all year

Das College Haus is a turn-of-the-century Greek Revival Victorian, located three blocks from Fredericksburg's historic Main Street. Guests enjoy the "at home" atmosphere as they relax on the porches or balcony with complimentary beverages and cookies. The entire home is beautifully appointed with antiques, original art and comfortable period furniture. The spacious guest bedrooms and suites have central heat and air, king or queen-size beds, sitting areas, room refrigerators, coffee makers, cable television and VCRs with videos available in the library. After Myrna's delicious breakfast in the dining room, guests may visit the studio of nationally known artist Tim Saska.

Historical Significance:

The house was built in 1916 by Ernest and Rossalia Grobe. It remained in the same family for almost seventy years until the death of their granddaughter, Ella Gold, in 1985. Miss Gold was a historian and educator and made a significant contribution to the community.

Places To Go, Sites To See:

There's something for everyone in Fredericksburg with its numerous museums, parks, shops, and frequent German festivals on the Marketplatz with music, dancing, and arts and crafts. For the outdoors person, a hike up Enchanted Rock, incredible sunsets, and abundant wildlife contribute to the magic of the Texas Hill Country.

Das Garten Haus

604 S. Washington
Fredericksburg, TX 78624

800-416-4287
830-990-8408
E-Mail: mac@hctc.net

Hosts: Lynn and Kevin
MacWithey

BEDS: 2 suites, 2 private baths

BREAKFAST & OTHER MEALS: Full breakfast

$$, $$$ Open all year

Lynn and Kevin MacWithey have created a traditional bed and breakfast with "old world charm" at Das Garten Haus. Their fifty-year-old home has fine oak and pine floors throughout, and beautiful crown molding in the formal rooms. Guest accommodations are in two private suites behind the house, one downstairs and one upstairs. They overlook a New Orleans style courtyard and perennial garden created by Kevin, a professional horticulturist. Both suites have private entrances, cable TV, queen-size beds, and kitchen facilities with complimentary beverages and snacks. Lynn and Kevin prepare sumptuous breakfasts utilizing fresh herbs and vegetables from their garden, and serve in their formal dining room.

Historical Significance:

Completed in 1951 by Herman August Adams, Das Garten Haus is a fine example of eclectic architecture. Building it as his retirement home, Adams included brick archways, porches, and paved garden areas. After his death, the home changed hands until purchased by the Ottmers, a prominent old family in Fredericksburg. It is still affectionately known as "the old Ottmer's place."

Places To Go, Sites To See:

Dine at The Nest, one of Fredericksburg's finest restaurants, located just across the street from Das Garten Haus. Visit the Nimitz Museum, climb Enchanted Rock, tour the vineyards. Sit in the garden and watch the butterflies. Relax by the pool at Baron's Creek Racquet Club where you'll have guest privileges.

The Delforge Place

710 Ettie Street
Fredericksburg, TX 78624

800-997-0462
830-997-6212
Fax: 830-990-8320
E-Mail: delplace@speakez.net
Website: www.speakez.net/delforgeplace/

Hosts: Betsy, George and Pete Delforge

BEDS: 1 room, 3 suites, 4 private baths

BREAKFAST & OTHER MEALS: Full breakfast

$$ Open all year, two night minimum on holidays and special events weekends

Betsy, George and Pete get accolades galore for offering a fine traditional bed and breakfast, among the first in Fredericksburg. The Delforge Place has been welcoming guests since 1985. Built in 1898, the home retains its character with original stained, beveled, and etched glass doors and windows, polished wood floors, 12-foot ceilings, and sparkling chandeliers. Exquisitely furnished with American, European, and Oriental heirlooms and antiques, the Delforge Place offers four spacious, historically-themed guest rooms with private baths; one with Jacuzzi. All reflect the family's heritage and sea captain ancestry. Guests will find special cookies in their rooms upon arrival and will feast on Betsy's memorable breakfasts, featured in *Gourmet* and *Bon Appetit* magazines.

Historical Significance:

Built in 1898 as a one-room "Sunday House," The Delforge Place is an excellent example of how these weekend homes grew over the years to become comfortable, elaborate residences for family members living in town full time.

Places To Go, Sites To See:

Drive Willow City Loop for incredible bluebonnet viewing, tour LBJ Ranch, visit the Admiral Nimitz Museum. Climb Enchanted Rock – take Betsy's "Special Day" picnic basket for fortification. Play horseshoes and croquet, or try your hand at archery on the grounds. Enjoy guest privileges at Baron's Creek Swim and Racquet Club.

Magnolia House

101 E. Hackberry
Fredericksburg, TX 78624

800-880-4374
830-997-0306
E-mail:
magnolia@hctc.net
Website:
www.magnolia-house.com

Hosts: Joyce and Pat Kennard

BEDS: 3 rooms, 2 suites, 5 private baths

BREAKFAST & OTHER MEALS: Full breakfast

$$, $$$ Open all year, two night minimum on holidays and special events weekends

This traditional bed and breakfast, known for gracious Southern hospitality, has a three diamond AAA rating. The elegant home and its five guest rooms (two are suites with fireplaces) are tastefully decorated with antiques and appointed with comfort in mind. The Kennards have thought of every detail — complimentary beverages and snacks, plush terry cloth robes, color television with premium channels. Guests enjoy the common areas and spacious porches as well as the stone patio with a fish pond and waterfall. Magnolia House's signature breakfast is served either in the dining room or breakfast room. Use of an off-site swim and tennis club that includes a workout facility is an added amenity.

Historical Significance:

In 1923, this stately home was designed and built for the Stein family. Edward Stein, architect and designer of the Gillespie County Courthouse, personally selected each piece of lumber to make this one of the most carefully constructed houses in the area. Restored in 1991, Magnolia House has been designated a Recorded Texas Historic Landmark.

Places To Go, Sites To See:

Fortify yourself with the bountiful southern breakfast before a day of golfing, hiking, or Main Street shopping. You can also visit one of the museums, wineries, or the LBJ ranch located fifteen miles east of Fredericksburg.

Metzger Sunday House

Gästehaus Schmidt
Reservation Service
231 W. Main
Fredericksburg, TX 78624

830-997-5612
E-Mail: gasthaus@ktc.com
Website:
www.ktc.net/GSchmidt/
metzger.htm

Owners: Knopp and Metzger

BEDS: Guest House - 1 bedroom, 1 bath

BREAKFAST & OTHER MEALS: Continental breakfast

$$ Open all year

This original Sunday House, still in the Metzger family, is located on a small knoll on San Antonio Street. In the heart of the historic district, only a block from Main Street, its location makes it perfect for relaxing after a busy day of shopping and sightseeing in Fredericksburg. The main room, lavishly decorated in pinks and hunter green, is both the bedroom and sitting room with a queen-size, antique high-back bed, velvet horsehair couch, and television. Many family heirlooms and mementos are displayed. The bath has a full tub and shower with an ample supply of plush towels and soaps. A fully equipped kitchen, delightful with bright, cheerful colors, contains a table and four chairs, a small range, microwave, and refrigerator with complimentary soft drinks, teas, and coffees.

Historical Significance:

The home was built in 1898 by John and Mathilda Schmidtzinsky Metzger to be used on weekends, as they lived 18 miles from town in Luckenbach. It was used as a home to attend church, shop, and for other in-town chores. This is the original structure.

Places To Go, Sites To See:

Enjoy tranquility in the porch swing, stroll by other nearby Sunday Houses, or visit the many attractions of Fredericksburg – museums, shops, parks, and eateries.

The Orchard Inn

Hwy. 87 South
Rt. 3, Box 115
Fredericksburg, TX 78624

800-439-4320
830-990-0257

E-Mail: orchard@fbg.net
Hosts: Annette and Mark Wieser

BEDS: 1 room, 3 suites, 1 cabin, 5 private baths

BREAKFAST & OTHER MEALS: Full or Continental Plus breakfast

$$, $$$ Open all year, two night minimum on holidays and special events weekends

Annette and Mark offer a unique country inn experience, just two minutes from downtown Fredericksburg. This farm has been in the Wieser family since 1928 and the original home was beautifully restored and expanded in 1997. It sits amid 50 acres with a peaceful pine grove surrounding a lake where guests may swim, canoe, and use the paddle boat. The home retains the original ceilings, floors, wine cellar, and exquisite gingerbread detailing. The interior is furnished with American, European, and Oriental antiques, family heirlooms, and original artwork. The König log cabin was built by German immigrants in 1870, moved to its present location on the property, and restored in 1992. Three spacious, luxury suites are scheduled for completion in early 1998.

Historical Significance:

The Inn's original structure was built in 1904 by Peter Bonn, an early German immigrant, on property purchased in 1846 by the German Immigration Company. The König cabin was the 1870's home for a German family, moved to its present location to save it from flooding along the Pedernales River. As the original retail peach outlet for Das Peach Haus, it became the cornerstone for Fischer & Wieser Specialty Foods.

Places To Go, Sites To See:

Inn guests are welcome to stroll about the 50-acre farm with pecan and peach orchards, enjoy the wildflowers, and feed the ducks and fish. Shop in Fredericksburg, tour the nearby LBJ Ranch, visit wildflower farms and local wineries, hike and climb in parks, and enjoy the good life.

The Schandua Suite

205 E. Main Street

Fredericksburg, TX 78624

888-990-1415
830-990-1415
E-Mail: sharla44@hctc.net

Hosts: Sharla and Jonathan Godfrey

BEDS: 1 suite, 1 private bath

BREAKFAST & OTHER MEALS: Continental Plus breakfast

$$$ Open all year, two night minimum on weekends

Sharla and Jonathan Godfrey have created an elegant guest suite upstairs in the 1897 Schandua Building, an oasis in the heart of the central shopping district. This spacious 1340-sq. ft. suite features a king-size bed, 12-foot ceilings, a complete Pullman kitchen, color cable televisions, telephone, and central air and heat. The luxurious suite is furnished with fine antiques throughout, and offers every imaginable amenity. A floor-to-ceiling library holds tales for every taste. Complimentary hors-d'oeuvres are served upon arrival, and a bountiful Continental breakfast, featuring fresh-baked German pastries, is left in the kitchen. Guests have a private back porch balcony overlooking a whimsical roof-top cactus garden and a lavishly landscaped, secluded courtyard at ground level.

Historical Significance:

Built in 1897 on an original townlot deeded by the German Emigration Company, The Schandua Building, made of hand-hewn native limestone, is a Recorded Texas Historic Landmark. For several generations the upstairs rooms served as a residence for the family who operated a hardware store downstairs. Today, The Schandua Suite occupies a portion of the original upstairs residence.

Places To Go, Sites To See:

The Schandua Suite is located in the center of Fredericksburg's celebrated shopping district. Just outside the door are exquisite shops, art galleries, and world-class dining, as well as unique museums, all within easy walking distance.

Schildknecht-Weidenfeller House

Gästehaus Schmidt
Reservation Service
231 W. Main
Fredericksburg, TX 78624

830-997-5612
Fax: 830-997-8282
E-Mail: gasthaus@ktc.com
Website:
www.speakez.net/schildknecht

Owners: Carter and Ellis Schildknecht

BEDS: Guest House - 4 bedrooms, 2 baths

BREAKFAST & OTHER MEALS: German Continental Plus breakfast

$$$ Open all year, two night minimum on weekends

The Schildknecht-Weidenfeller House is located in the heart of Fredericksburg's historic district. This 1870s German limestone house, with high ceilings, thick stone walls, and pine plank flooring, rents as one unit housing up to ten people. Carter's desire to please her guests is evident throughout – wood for the fireplace, natural cotton bed linens, phone, cable television, central heat and air, and a fully equipped kitchen. From the original loft-turned-master suite to the cellar, the house is decorated with carefully-chosen primitive antiques and handmade quilts and has been featured in *Country Decorating Ideas* magazine. A German-style breakfast is left to enjoy in private at your leisure. A quote from the guest comment book declares, "Pure unadulterated Heaven!…Thanks for what must be the best place on the planet!"

Historical Significance:

Built in the 1870s on property Johann Weidenfeller purchased for "consideration of one hundred and twenty-five coin dollars," this sturdy limestone structure housed a member of Weidenfeller's family until 1970 and is often on tours of historic homes in Fredericksburg.

Places To Go, Sites To See:

Replace busy urban lives with quiet, relaxing moments – in rockers on the front porch, in the large, shaded yard, or on cool winter evenings in front of the fireplace.

Schmidt Barn

Gästehaus Schmidt
Reservation Service
231 W. Main
Fredericksburg, TX 78624

830-997-5612
E-Mail: gasthaus@ktc.com
Website:
www.ktc.net/GSchmidt/
schmibn.htm

Hosts: Charles and Loretta Schmidt

BEDS: Guest House - 1 bedroom, 1 bath

BREAKFAST & OTHER MEALS: German Continental Plus breakfast

$$ Open all year, two night minimum on holidays and special events weekends

Old World ambiance and warm hospitality fill the Schmidt Barn, located next to Charles and Loretta's home. Thick stone walls and milled timber beams maintain century-old charm in the living and dining areas. The bathroom invites guests to relish a long, slow soak in a most unconventional sunken brick tub. A loft bedroom provides a cozy sleeping place. Heirloom quilts, antique linens, samplers, and a collection of vintage toys enliven the wooden-beamed room. Representative of the area's early heritage, this enchanting guest house in its country setting with flower and herb gardens could easily transport guests to another century. Perhaps that explains why The Schmidt Barn has been featured in countless magazine articles and as a cover story in *Country Living*.

Historical Significance:

The remnants of an old limestone rock barn were lovingly saved to turn this 1860s building into a charming guest house. The Barn and the Schmidt's home sit on land that was granted to some of the first German immigrants settling Fredericksburg.

Places To Go, Sites To See:

Guests may enjoy all the attractions of Fredericksburg, only five minutes away, but will probably rather return home to country quiet, a swing for two under an ancient oak tree, and the solitude, peace, and romance of their own making.

Settlers Crossing

104 Settlers Crossing Road
Fredericksburg, TX 78624

800-874-1020
830-997-2722

Website: www.settlerscrossing.com

Hosts: David and Judy Bland

BEDS: Guest Houses - 7 houses, 7 private baths

BREAKFAST & OTHER MEALS: Continental Plus breakfast

$$, $$$ Open all year

A grand country estate, Settlers Crossing offers a unique blend of charm and luxury. Its special spirit has been captured in recent articles in *Country Home* and *Country Living* magazines. Judy and David occupy "Richland," a stately Kentucky plantation home, circa 1790, on the property. Guests choose from seven private historic guest houses, each furnished with 18th and 19th-century country antiques and queen or king-size beds. Six have fireplaces and four have Jacuzzi tubs. Each house is rented separately and can accommodate from two to six guests. The homes are spread over 35 park-like acres of towering oaks, rolling pastures, and flower gardens with Settlers Creek meandering through. Guests enjoy the resident mascot, Buster the donkey, and a flock of Russian Romanoff sheep roaming free.

Historical Significance:

Four of the guest houses at Settlers Crossing are part of the original homestead which was home to four generations of the same Texas family. The Kusenberger log cabin, now a guest house, was built in 1850 and is the oldest home built by the Germans outside Fredericksburg.

Places To Go, Sites To See:

Although Settlers Crossing is just five minutes from all the attractions of Fredericksburg, a stay here clearly favors absolute languor and dreams of a slower lifestyle.

Watkins Hill

608 East Creek Street
Fredericksburg, TX 78624

800-899-1672
830-997-6739

Owner: Edgar Watkins Trust

BEDS: 4 rooms, 8 suites, 12 private baths

BREAKFAST & OTHER MEALS: Full breakfast delivered to rooms in wicker baskets; private party arrangements available

$$$ Open all year

Watkins Hill is a 1 ½ -acre compound of buildings and gardens overlooking a creek and field of Longhorns, one block from Main Street. The main building, a 7,000 sq. ft. edifice, contains four guest rooms, a parlor with fireplace, conservatory, library with fireplace, and an enormous meeting room in an 1840 log barn. Each guest room has a private entrance, porch, butler's pantry stocked with complimentary refreshments, 18th and 19th-century antique furnishings, elaborately-canopied beds, individual heat and air, television, VCR, telephone, ceiling fan, and designer linens. Most have cathedral ceilings and fireplaces. A hot gourmet breakfast is delivered to the guest room door.

Historical Significance:

Four of the seven buildings at Watkins Hill date from the 19th century. These include a massive 1835 log house, an even larger 1840 log barn, an 1890s farm building and Watkins Hill's premier accommodations, the four-room, four fireplace stone Basse-Burrier house of 1855. The other buildings are turn-of-the-century style using pre-Civil War lumber and architectural elements.

Places To Go, Sites To See:

Each room contains a special Watkins Hill directory of recommended shops, drives, cafes, and galleries.

The Yellow House

Gästehaus Schmidt
Reservation Service
231 W. Main Street
Fredericksburg, TX 78624

830-997-5612
Website:
w w w . k t c . n e t / G S c h m i d t /
yellow.htm

Owners: Donna and Dan Mittel

BEDS: Guest House — 1 bedroom, 1 bath

BREAKFAST & OTHER MEALS: Continental Plus breakfast

$$ Open all year, two night minimum on event weekends

This home has been described as an adult-sized doll house. Built at the turn of the century as an original Sunday House, it is located two blocks from Main Street. It has always been known as the "little yellow house under the big oak tree." The bedroom/sitting room is decorated in pale dusty rose with delicate lace curtains. Plate racks with "grandmother's cabbage rose" china and two comfortable wingback chairs create the feel of yesteryear. The four-poster queen-size bed sits high off the floor. A generous continental breakfast, featuring German pastries, is left in the kitchen which is fully equipped with a refrigerator, microwave, stove, and coffee maker. Guests may enjoy privileges at Baron's Creek Swim & Tennis Club.

Historical Significance:

Built around 1900 as a Sunday House by Oma Stein after her husband died. It was built close to the Catholic church because two of Mrs. Stein's daughters were nuns. Although Sunday Houses usually have an outside staircase, this one had an inside staircase so her grandchildren would not have to get wet or cold.

Places To Go, Sites To See:

The Yellow House is located just two blocks from Main Street with its multitude of shops and restaurants. Visitors may enjoy easy day excursions to nearby Enchanted Rock or the LBJ Ranch.

Inn on the River

205 S.W. Barnard Street
Glen Rose, TX 76043

800-575-2101
972-424-7119
Fax: 972-424-9766

Host: Kathi Thompson

BEDS: 22 rooms, 22 private baths

BREAKFAST & OTHER MEALS: Full breakfast; four-course gourmet dinners on Friday and Saturday nights by reservation, other nights for groups with prior arrangement

$$$ Open all year

A recorded Texas Historic Landmark, Inn On The River is one of the largest country inns in Texas. Nestled along the banks of the Paluxy River, the Inn offers casual elegance in a charming and peaceful environment with gourmet food and personalized service. Guest rooms are appointed with antiques, fine European linens, featherbeds and goose down comforters. Breakfast is served in the glassed-in dining room overlooking a vast expanse of lawn gently sloping to meet the river. A fully-equipped conference center is available for corporate meetings and executive retreats.

Historical Significance:

Inn On The River's two-story structure was built by Dr. George P. Synder in 1916, as a "drugless sanatorium." People came from across the nation for the curative mineral baths and healthy food offered for renewal and rejuvenation. Eighty years later, guests of the Inn still visit for renewal and rejuvenation.

Places To Go, Sites To See:

Golf at Squaw Valley, take a jeep tour of Fossil Rim Wildlife Center, fish on Lake Granbury, canoe down the Brazos River, enjoy live performances at the Granbury Opera House. "The Promise", a play depicting the life of Christ, is performed in the Amphitheatre each year on Friday and Saturday evenings, June through October.

The Houston House Bed & Breakfast

621 E. Saint George Street
Gonzales, TX 78629

888-477-0760
830-672-6940
830-672-6097
Fax: 830-672-6228
E-Mail: hhouse@connecti.com
Website: www.houstonhouse.com

Hosts: Gene and Diana Smith

BEDS: 5 rooms, 5 private baths

BREAKFAST & OTHER MEALS: Full breakfast; candlelight dinners, teas, luncheons with prior arrangement, weddings and other special occasions

$$, $$$ Open all year

The Houston House is a Queen Anne Victorian mansion renowned for its architectural detail, towers, and wrap-around porches. The interior showcases original parquet floors, fireplaces, and embossed ceilings and features longleaf pine woodwork on towering pillars at the parlor entrance, on the magnificent staircase in the foyer, on the massive pocket doors, and on the decorative paneling. Hand-painted murals that adorn the parlor ceiling and dining room walls were painted by Will Houston's wife, Sue, who studied art in Europe. The Houston House is furnished throughout with antiques, most dating to the time of the Civil War. Guest bedrooms offer telephones, cable television, and VCRs. A scrumptious breakfast may feature Diana's Bavarian pancakes. Lucky guests get a tour of the town in one of Gene's antique cars.

Historical Significance:

Built in 1895 for William Buchner Houston, a well-known cattleman, The Houston House is one of many imposing homes built in Gonzales from the 1880s through the 1920s.

Places To Go, Sites To See:

Gonzales earned its place in history when, on October 2, 1835, the first shot was fired for Texas Independence. The area is exceedingly rich in Texas history and recently the movie location for *TRUE WOMEN*, based on the novel about pioneer Texas women set in the areas of Gonzales, Seguin, and San Marcos.

St. James Inn

723 St. James
Gonzales, TX 78629

830-672-7066

Hosts: Ann and J.R. Covert

BEDS: 6 rooms, 5 private baths

BREAKFAST & OTHER MEALS: Full breakfast; candlelight dinners, getaway packages, and picnic baskets available with advance reservations

$$ Open all year

J.R. and Ann opened this former cattle baron's mansion in 1989 to invite Bed & Breakfast guests to share its rich history. The home has exceptionally large rooms, fireplaces and porches. The Coverts found the original plans for the home and have followed them as closely as possible in their renovations. Ann has tastefully furnished the home with period antiques and guest's relaxation and comfort in mind. Several rooms are named for their original residents and reflect their personalities. Family heirlooms and memorabilia create an ambiance reminiscent of another era. A delicious breakfast might include "mile-high" French pancakes, delicate Southern crepes, or other specialties.

Historical Significance:

Built as a family home in 1914, the St. James Inn is of Greek Revival architecture with three floors, nine working fireplaces, and is a testament to the wealth of cattle baron Walter Kokernot. Walter was the grandson of D.L. Kokernot who was granted several leagues of land in Gonzales County for his heroic service in the Texas Revolution.

Places To Go, Sites To See:

As the "Lexington of Texas," Gonzales is steeped in history. Museums bulge with artifacts and memories of the beginning of Texas. Browse antique shops or take one of Ann's "food treasure" picnic baskets to a park and enjoy the scenery or sunset.

The Captain's House on the Lake

123 West Doyle Street
Granbury, TX 76048

817-579-6664
817-579-LAKE

Hosts: Julia and Bob Pannell

BEDS: 2 suites, 1 room, 3 private baths

BREAKFAST & OTHER MEALS: Continental Plus breakfast tray to room and special menu for brunch or lunch at the historic bakery on the square

$$$ Open all year, two night minimum during holidays or festivals

Overlooking Lake Granbury, The Captain's House was lovingly restored by current owners, Julia and Bob Pannell. This stunning Queen Anne features splendid Victorian-era decor, original stained-glass windows, and a parlor mantel, designed in the 1870-1890 period style, handmade by the Pannell's son, Craig. One-of-a-kind handmade carpets designed by Julia cover some of the original floors, yet leave much of the 1874 oak and pine wood beauty. Accommodations are located upstairs around the Common Room with its cable TV, books dating to the 1800s, and refreshment area with sumptuous desserts. Each guest room has a private bath, fresh flowers, and is tastefully appointed with memories — precious dolls, wedding dresses, steamer trunks. A balcony overlooks the lake and offers a backstairs entrance.

Historical Significance:

This elegant Queen Anne Victorian home was built in 1874-75 by James H. Doyle, affectionately nicknamed "Captain," a respected community leader and early mayor. The first recorded house on Doyle Street, it served as the site of many social events during the early years in Granbury's history. About 85% of the original outside structure and windows remain today.

Places To Go, Sites To See:

This B&B is only two blocks from Granbury's Historic Square with its antique and gift shops, great restaurants, Opera House, and nationally renown Great Race Hall of Fame Museum. The area offers a huge variety of activities; The Captain's House offers pampered service.

The Iron Horse Inn

616 Thorp Spring Rd.
Granbury, TX 76048

817-579-5535
Website:
www.theironhorseinn.com

Hosts: Bob and Judy Atkinson

BEDS: 2 rooms, 5 suites, 7 private baths

BREAKFAST & OTHER MEALS: Full breakfast

$$, $$$ Open all year, two night minimum on holidays and special events weekends

The Iron Horse Inn is a carefully restored, elegant 1905 Craftsman style home situated on an acre of landscaped grounds amid huge pecan and live oak trees. Original beveled and leaded glass, distinctive maple wood floors, 12-foot ceilings, an inviting front porch, two comfortable living rooms, and rich hand-crafted woodwork are part of the charm of this 7,000 sq. ft. historic home, the largest in Granbury. A variety of accommodations offer guests quite a choice: one elegant suite has French doors opening into a solarium with thirteen antique windows; one creates the atmosphere of a 1920's ocean liner suite, complete with authentic ship's door with a porthole; and one is the limestone-walled wine cellar. A sumptuous breakfast is served in the formal dining room.

Historical Significance:

This "ultimate bungalow," designed for Daniel Cogdell by famed architect Wyatt Hedrick, contained many innovations including a central heating system, retractable blade ceiling fan, and bathroom skylight. President of the local bank, Mr. Cogdell also owned cotton gins, rock quarries, land, cattle, and was responsible for bringing the railroad to Granbury.

Places To Go, Sites To See:

The Iron Horse Inn is just a few blocks from Granbury's Opera House on the historic courthouse square, antique and gift shops, great restaurants, and the shore of Lake Granbury.

Pearl Street Inn Bed & Breakfast

319 W. Pearl Street
Granbury, TX 76048

888-PearlSt (732-7578)
817-579-7465
E-mail: danette@itexas.net
Website:
www2.itexas.net/~danette

Host: Danette D. Hebda

BEDS: 5 rooms, 5 private baths

BREAKFAST & OTHER MEALS: Full breakfast; Dinners for six or more available with advance reservations

$$, $$$ Open all year

Guests are invited to relax in stately, stylish comfort only two blocks from Granbury's historic square. Pearl Street Inn offers comfortable, antique-appointed guest rooms with king-size beds and private baths. The English Garden suite, in soft shades of peach and green with ivy-papered bathroom walls, features a spacious sitting room/sunroom. Breakfast is served in the formal dining room. Danette delights in creating personalized service for her guests. Inquire about the "Enchanted Evening" package, a unique romantic experience. Enjoy the year-round outdoor hot tub. Experience a special stay where "days move gently in all seasons."

Historical Significance:

This Foursquare Prairie style home, built in 1911, is known historically as the B.M. Estes House. Representative of the Arts & Crafts movement, it features wide eaves, large square porch supports, pocket doors, Victorian touches, and a massive front door.

Places To Go, Sites To See:

Granbury is a popular tourist destination. Enjoy live theater at the Granbury Opera House, Dinosaur Valley State Park, golf, drive-in movies, water activities, "The Promise" Amphitheater, historical landmarks, Fossil Rim Wildlife Park, the immense variety of shops and restaurants on the square, and year-round local festivals.

Gruene Country Homestead Inn

832 Gruene Road
New Braunfels, TX 78130

830-606-0216
E-Mail:
homestead@compuvision.net
Website: www.io.com/
GrueneHomesteadInn

Hosts: E.G. and Billie Miles

BEDS: 10 rooms, 5 suites, 15 private baths

BREAKFAST & OTHER MEALS: Continental Plus breakfast

$$, $$$ Open all year, two night minimum on weekends and holidays

Gruene Country Homestead Inn is a stone's throw from the Gruene Historic District and the Guadalupe River. It offers a variety of roomy suites in renovated farmhouses, cottages, and barns from another era. Several rooms are in an 1850s vintage structure of adobe, cedar beams, and barn wood, constructed by German settlers. Enjoy the luxuries of today with whirlpool baths, personal coffee makers, king or queen-sized beds, private sitting areas, wet bars, refrigerators, and televisions. Hanz Halle, a renovated barn, makes a perfect place for meetings, retreats, or receptions. Outside, guests can enjoy the swimming pool, landscaped gardens, or just the peace of this haven of tranquility in the beautiful Texas Hill Country.

Historical Significance:

Buildings at the Inn are renovated and restored early Texas structures of varying architectural styles constructed in the late 1800s and early 1900s. The Fachwerk style farmhouse built in 1860 is the original building on the site.

Places To Go, Sites To See:

Gruene Country Homestead Inn is close to all the attractions of historic Gruene and New Braunfels, the Guadalupe and Comal Rivers, and Schlitterbahn Water Park.

Gruene Mansion Inn

1275 Gruene Road
New Braunfels, TX 78130

830-629-2641
Fax: 830-629-7375
E-Mail: gruenemansion@gruene.net
Website: www.gruene.net/gruenemansion/

Hosts: Bill and Sharon McCaskill

BEDS: 28 rooms, 28 private baths

BREAKFAST & OTHER MEALS: Breakfast is optional for overnight guests at $5 per person; full service restaurant offers fine European cuisine for lunch and dinner

$$, $$$ Open all year, two night minimum on weekends

The centerpiece of this historic complex is H.D. Gruene's Eastlake Victorian home built on a bluff overlooking the Guadalupe River. Most guest accommodations are in restored original 1870s outbuildings and barns from Mr. Gruene's cotton plantation. Appointed in a style Sharon calls "Victorian rustic elegance," a combination of antiques, Ralph Lauren fabrics and linens, and handmade furniture in a rustic setting, all rooms have private baths with deep, old-fashioned tubs and pedestal sinks. Many have private decks overlooking the Guadalupe River. An optional gourmet breakfast is served in the mansion's dining room.

Historical Significance:

City founder, Heinrich D. Gruene established his cotton plantation, built his mansion, the dance hall, the cotton gin, and most of this town in the 1870s. Listed in the National Register of Historic Places, Gruene Mansion Inn is also a Recorded Texas Historic Landmark.

Places To Go, Sites To See:

Located in the heart of the Gruene Historic District, this Inn makes a perfect base for exploring the tremendous variety of quaint shops and restaurants and endless opportunities for river rafting and water activities. Gruene Hall, Texas' oldest dance hall, regularly offers celebrity entertainment.

Angel Arbor Bed & Breakfast Inn

848 Heights Boulevard
Houston, TX 77007

800-722-8788
713-868-4654

Fax: 713-861-3189
E-mail: b-bhoutx@wt.net
Website:
www.angelarbor.com

Hosts: Marguerite and Dean Swanson

BEDS: 3 rooms, 1 suite, 4 private baths

BREAKFAST & OTHER MEALS: Full breakfast; Murder Mystery dinner parties

$$, $$$, Open all year

This Georgian style inn derives its name from the two primary features of the backyard garden: a lovely angel statue, and a vine-covered arbor. The first floor boasts an antique-filled parlor, reading room, gracious formal dining room, and sunroom. A wicker-furnished solarium overlooks the manicured garden. Four spacious accommodations, each with an angel-inspired name, fulfill the promise of a heavenly night's rest. Tastefully furnished, each has a queen-size bed, cable television, telephone, and a private bath with luxury soaps, lotions, and bathrobes; two feature whirlpool tubs for two. Guests enjoy a memorable, formally served breakfast. Well known for her innovative Murder Mystery dinner parties, Marguerite pampered guests for many years at Durham House. Now she and Dean welcome visitors to Angel Arbor.

Historical Significance:

This stately red brick home was built in 1923, on fashionable Houston Heights Boulevard, for John and Katherine McTighe. Known historically as the McTighe-Durham house, possibly its more noted resident was the second owner, Jay L. Durham, the first fire chief of Houston Heights.

Places To Go, Sites To See:

Located five minutes from downtown Houston, Angel Arbor satisfies honeymooners as well as business travelers with its pleasing blend of convenience and luxury.

The Whistler Bed & Breakfast — Eastham/Thomason Home

906 Avenue M
Huntsville, TX 77340

800-404-2834 or
409-295-2834
From Houston: 800-432-1288
or 713-965-0311

Host: Mary Thomason Clegg

BEDS: 5 rooms, 4 private baths, 1 shared bath

BREAKFAST & OTHER MEALS: Full breakfast

$$, $$$ Open all year

This Recorded Texas Historic Landmark mansion is Mary's family home, nestled among enormous trees on three acres of landscaped grounds. She carefully restored it out of love and named it for her grandfather, whose whistling was one of her earliest childhood memories. Two blocks from the Courthouse Square, The Whistler has a welcoming ambiance that invites serenity. Rest on the large veranda, or curl up in front of one of the five fireplaces. Lavishly furnished with original antiques and family heirlooms, guest rooms offer nostalgic charm with luxurious modern comforts. Mary serves a bountiful breakfast in the dining room on a rosewood table made from a piano which survived the Civil War. She will tell that story, along with many others, to interested guests.

Historical Significance:

For four generations, this stately mansion has been the home of two major Walker County pioneer families: the Thomasons and the Easthams, paternal and maternal ancestors of the current owner. Recorded in the Texas Family Land Heritage Register, The Whistler, built in 1859, is one of the earliest homes in Walker County still occupied.

Places To Go, Sites To See:

The Sam Houston Museum, Sam Houston State University, Sam Houston National Forest, Sam Houston's home and burial site plus the recently built 76-foot statue of Sam Houston pay tribute to this Texas hero.

Pride House

409 Broadway
Jefferson, TX 75657

800-894-3526
903-665-2675
Fax: 903-665-3901
E-mail: jefftx@mind.net
Website: www.jeffersontexas.com

Hosts: Carol Abernathy and
Christel Frederick

BEDS: 10 rooms, 10 private baths

BREAKFAST & OTHER MEALS: Full breakfast

$$, $$$ Open all year

Pride House consists of a Victorian mansion (the Main House) and its original servants quarters (the Dependency). This Jefferson landmark home features 12-foot ceilings, four fireplaces, and the original woodwork, hardware, and stained glass windows in every room. Both houses are furnished with antiques, heirlooms, and original art, and provide such amenities as imported soaps, bath sheets and hairdryers. The Dependency has low ceilings and a country decor. Its rooms have private entrances and porches or balconies. Snacks and hot or cold drinks are always available. Breakfasts feature such signature recipes such as Praline Pears, Eggs Galveston, and Jefferson Pecan Coffee.

Historical Significance:

This Recorded Texas Historic Landmark, built in 1888 by lumber baron George Brown, was the first Bed and Breakfast in Texas. Constructed in the stick Victorian style, it features magnificent stained glass windows and gingerbread trim.

Places To Go, Sites To See:

Once a bustling steamboat port, Jefferson is now a charming, quiet little town with brick streets, picket fences, magnificent historic homes, dozens of antique shops, great eateries, museums, horse-drawn carriage rides, river tours, and a real steamboat ride on moss-draped Caddo Lake. Jefferson offers unique and wonderful tours of many fine historic homes.

The Terry-McKinnon House

109 W. Henderson
Jefferson, TX 75657

903-665-1933
Fax: 903-665-9003
E-Mail:
71663,655 (Compuserve)

Hosts: Ted and Kay McKinnon

BEDS: 4 rooms, 4 private baths

BREAKFAST & OTHER MEALS: Full breakfast

$$, $$$ Open all year, two night minimum for holidays and special events

East Texas hospitality reigns supreme in this traditional bed and breakfast. Built in 1880, this grand home retains many original features, including the magnificent oak stairway, unusual beaded dining room walls, pine plank flooring, 14-foot ceilings, brilliant chandeliers, and coal burning fireplaces in every room except the kitchen. The home is furnished with lovely antiques and collectibles, and the bedrooms display treasured family quilts on king or queen-size beds. Kay serves a gourmet breakfast which may feature such delights as praline bacon, sticky buns, herb baked eggs and fresh fruit.

Historical Significance:

This excellent example of Gothic Revival was built in 1880 by cotton factor S.D. Rainey for his family. Purchased in 1886 by Mary Terry, the home remained in her family until 1994. It has been extensively renovated while maintaining the architectural integrity.

Places To Go, Sites To See:

Located downtown, The Terry-McKinnon House is convenient to the many attractions of historic Jefferson: antique and gift shops, horse drawn carriage rides, guided tour trolley rides, historic home tours, Excelsior Hotel tour, Texas Heritage Archives/Library, Historical Jefferson Museum, Cypress Bayou Railroad rides, Caddo Lake boat tours, and fine dining for lunch or dinner.

Bed & Breakfast On The Bay

701 Bay Avenue
Kemah, TX 77565

281-334-4141

Hosts: Mary Patterson
and son,
Pat Patterson

BEDS: 8 rooms, 2 suites, 10 private baths

BREAKFAST & OTHER MEALS: Full breakfast

$, $$, $$$ Open all year

Three diverse properties compose this B&B on Galveston Bay. The Crews Quarters, a 1930s "Cape Cod" bayside cottage, features balconies and an excellent view of the bay. This cozy, comfortable three-bedroom cottage offers ideal accommodations for families. The Captains Quarters is an outstanding reproduction of an 1880s New England sea captain's house. Elegantly furnished in antiques and featuring nautical decor, some of the guest rooms have fireplaces and bay views. Guests enjoy a panoramic view and gentle sea breezes from two porches and a Widow's Walk. The 1874 Kipp House offers two enormous luxury suites overlooking Galveston Bay. This home features a screened front porch at water's edge and huge windows the full length of the upstairs suite. A sumptuous breakfast is served to all guests in the Captains Quarters' formal dining room.

Historical Significance:

The Crews Quarters was Mary's family beach house, built by her father in the 1930s. The 1874 Kipp House was built by John Kipp, one of the founding fathers of the town of Kemah. Built almost entirely of cypress wood brought in by boat, it has survived a number of hurricanes.

Places To Go, Sites To See:

Explore the bayside town of Kemah with its great variety of marinas and water activities, picturesque shops, and seafood restaurants.

The Luckenbach Inn

Old Luckenbach Road
Luckenbach, TX 78624

800-997-1124
830-997-2205
Fax: 830-997-1115
E-mail:
theinn@luckenbachtx.com
Website: www.luckenbachtx.com

Hosts: Eva & Capt. Matthew
Carinhas

BEDS: 6 rooms, 4 private baths, 1 shared bath

BREAKFAST & OTHER MEALS: Full breakfast; Catering available for weddings, family reunions and special occasions

$$, $$$ Open all year, two night minimum on holidays and special events weekends

Relax in rustic elegance and watch the stunning variety of resident birds. Guests are welcome to wander eleven secluded acres with 200-year-old cypress trees and a deep water creek, or ask Matt about fishing. Lounging on the porch until dark, when thousands of twinkling stars appear, is also a popular pastime. These charming country accommodations occupy an 1860s two story log cabin, a native limestone home, a private cottage over the wine cellar, and a two-story farmhouse. Steeped in history, the restored vintage buildings display longleaf pine floors and exposed log beams. Guest rooms offer comforts such as central heat and air and queen-size beds; all are decorated in soothing colors, and some have fireplaces, Jacuzzis, and kitchens. An abundant gourmet country breakfast is served daily.

Historical Significance:

The log cabin homestead of Luckenbach's founder, Jacob Kunz, was built in the mid 1860s. The local community gathered here for socializing, butchering, and the trading of goods.

Places To Go, Sites To See:

Located one-half mile from Luckenbach (pop. 25) and its legendary Dance Hall and Saloon, made famous by Waylon and Willie, the Luckenbach Inn is only nine minutes from bustling Fredericksburg.

Captain Shepard's Inn

Avenue D and 2nd St.
Marathon, TX 79842

800-884-4243

Hosts: Bill and Laurie
Stevens

BEDS: 5 rooms, 1 carriage house, 6 private baths

BREAKFAST & OTHER MEALS: Continental Plus breakfast

$$, $$$ Open all year

Captain Shepard's Inn has five large bedrooms, each with access to private porches. All are tastefully furnished with period antiques, some feature queen-size beds; one has a Jacuzzi. Guests may use two comfortable sitting rooms with a television and telephone, dining room, kitchen, and washer and dryer. The rich, dark varnished woodwork is unexpected in this rustic, arid region. The Carriage House has two bedrooms, one bathroom, and a sitting room with kitchenette and fireplace. Breakfast is not included for Carriage House guests. Captain Shepard's Inn is managed by The Gage Hotel and although physically removed from The Gage by a three-minute walk, all hotel facilities, including the pool, are available to Inn guests.

Historical Significance:

A former sea captain, Albion Shepard came to Marathon as a surveyor for the Southern Pacific Railroad in 1881. He stayed on to lay out town lots, establish the first post office, and become the first Postmaster. Owner of a large sheep ranch to the north, Shepard built a large two-story adobe home in 1899 which has been continuously occupied since its completion. Today, it is owned by Russ Tidwell of Austin and operated by the Gage Hotel.

Places To Go, Sites To See:

Marathon is the gateway to Big Bend National Park to the south and the Davis Mountains to the northwest.

The Gage Hotel

102 West Hwy. 90
Marathon, TX 79842

800-884-GAGE
Fax: 915-386-4510

Hosts: Bill and Laurie
Stevens

BEDS: 37 beds, 29 private baths, 8 shared baths

BREAKFAST & OTHER MEALS: None included; full service restaurant on premises

$, $$, $$$ Open all year

Perhaps no area of Texas is as unspoiled as the Trans-Pecos. Representing the diverse cultures of the Big Bend, The Gage guest rooms are decorated with Mexican primitive, Spanish colonial, and regional ranch period furnishings and artifacts. Guests may relax in the placita (courtyard), laze under the shade ramada, or swim in the large pool. Guest rooms are comfortably furnished, some have working fireplaces. Facilities and services are available for a full range of catered events including weddings, reunions, and corporate retreats. Café Cenizo serves excellent regional specialties such as cabrito and lamb chops as well as choice beef steaks; it offers a full bar and Texas-based wine list. Gage Tours can provide professionally guided van tours, river trips, and nature excursions.

Historical Significance:

Alfred Gage, a prosperous banker, businessman, and rancher from San Antonio made frequent trips to Marathon to check on his 500,000-acre ranch. In 1927, he built a hotel that would serve as his operation's headquarters while he was there. In 1982, the once-bustling, later neglected hotel was restored to recreate the atmosphere of cattle-dominated Trans-Pecos at the turn of the century.

Places To Go, Sites To See:

Marathon is the gateway to Big Bend National Park to the south and the Davis Mountains to the northwest.

Countryside Inn

¼ mile CR 103 East
P.O. Box 178
Martindale, TX 78655

512-357-2550
Fax: 512-357-2550

Host: Mary Ann Jones

BEDS: 3 rooms, 2 private baths, 1 shared bath

BREAKFAST & OTHER MEALS: Full breakfast

$$ Open weekends; open holidays and weekdays by request

This charming historic horse-trot home, built in 1874, sits in a peaceful country setting. Enjoy quiet walks to the river or cool beverages under the trees. The interior of the home has original soft pine floors, fireplaces, brick walls, and cedar thresholds, gorgeous even after a hundred and twenty years. Tastefully furnished in French country style, Countryside Inn is comfortable, warm, and inviting. Downstairs, the Jesse Jennings guest room features a 12-foot ceiling, king-size brass bed, TV/VCR, fireplace, sitting area , and private bath. Two dormer rooms upstairs share a bath and sitting room and are perfect for families or couples traveling together. The Sunrise Suite is a one-bedroom suite with a queen-size bed,TV/VCR, private bath, and sitting room. Outside porches overlook the back and side yards. Mary Ann serves an excellent country-style breakfast.

Historical Significance:

Reputed to be one of the first brick homes built south of Austin, the home is pale yellow stucco over the original brick. The original well stands in the yard as does the ancient cistern — reminders of early times. Countryside Inn was featured on the San Marcos Heritage Tour of Distinction in 1992.

Places To Go, Sites To See:

This home is conveniently situated near San Marcos, New Braunfels, historic Gruene, and Wimberley, as well as the San Marcos, Blanco, Guadalupe, and Comal rivers. Enjoy bird watching, toobing, canoeing, golf, outlet mall shopping, and antiquing.

Munzesheimer Manor

202 N. Newsom
Mineola, TX 75773

888-569-6634
903-569-6634
Fax: 903-569-9940
E-Mail:
RWMurray@prodigy.net

Hosts: Bob and Sherry Murray

BEDS: 7 rooms, 7 private baths

BREAKFAST & OTHER MEALS: Full breakfast

$$ Open all year

Bob and Sherry totally restored this 1898 Victorian mansion in 1987 to offer guests a special place "Where Time Stands Still." The splendid home features seven fireplaces with antique mantels, bay windows, and period antique furnishings. A large wrap-around porch overlooking the garden creates an ambiance of peace and serenity. Seven guest rooms, four upstairs in the main house and three in cottages on the side lawn, have central heat and air, ceiling fans, and private baths with footed tubs. Victorian gowns and nightshirts are provided, along with fresh flowers and sparkling cider, in each room. Morning coffee is delivered to your door, followed by a gourmet breakfast served in the formal dining room.

Historical Significance:

Built in 1898 by a German immigrant, Gustav Munzesheimer, this magnificent example of Princess Anne architecture is constructed entirely of pine and cedar, truly a fine testimony to the Victorian era. The Munzesheimers were merchants and leaders in the community during the late 1800s.

Places To Go, Sites To See:

This charming East Texas inn is conveniently located near numerous antique and craft shops, restaurants, state parks and lakes, golf courses, blueberry orchards, and Christmas Tree farms, as well as rose gardens, dogwood and azalea trails, a pottery factory, and a little theater group.

Noble Manor

411 E. Kilpatrick
Mineola, TX 75773

903-569-5720
Fax: 903-569-0472

Hosts: Rick and Shirley
Gordon

BEDS: 5 rooms, 3 suites, 1 cottage, 9 private baths

BREAKFAST & OTHER MEALS: Full breakfast

$$, $$$ Open all year except Thanksgiving and Christmas Days

Noble Manor retains the stately elegance and integrity of this historic home while offering amenities such as central heat and air and private baths, added during its three-year refurbishment. Original hardwood floors throughout have been restored, and vintage chandeliers illuminate the spacious common rooms. The guest rooms, suites, and private cottage with hot tub, are all appointed with antiques and fine linens, and feature individual coffee service. Shirley and Rick advise guests to "be sure to pack a lot of time in your overnight bag" to linger and enjoy their extensive library, wrap-around porch, and manicured gardens. Leisurely gourmet breakfasts are served on fine china in the formal dining room.

Historical Significance:

Representative of Classical Revival architecture, the nineteen-room mansion was built for Dr. Samuel Cloud Noble and his family in 1910. Using lumber cut and milled in Wood County, the construction spanned three years. A dance card signed by "Dr. Cloud" is a memento of past festivities in the third floor ballroom.

Places To Go, Sites To See:

Walk to the historic downtown area with its antique shops, art studios, theatre/playhouse, restaurants, and concert parlor. The same railroad tracks that gave rise to this town in the 1800s now host Amtrak's Texas Eagle.

The Castle Inn

1403 East Washington
Navasota, TX 77868

800-661-4346
409-825-8051

Hosts: Joyce and Gene Daniel

BEDS: 4 rooms, 4 private baths

BREAKFAST & OTHER MEALS: Full breakfast, private dinners with advance reservation

$$$ Open all year, two night minimum on A&M football game weekends

Guests enter this elegant Victorian mansion through a wrap-around porch enclosed with 110 panes of beveled glass. Interesting features include an original 20-foot stained glass window in the entry, nine half-bay windows resulting in octagonal rooms, and a "jealous husband" icebox. The widely-traveled hosts have furnished their home with fine antiques and cherished mementos. A spool staircase leads to the guest bedrooms, each with a private bath and appointed with Victorian-era furnishings. Fourteen-foot pocket doors open into the dining room where breakfast is served on china and crystal. Joyce describes it as a "down home" Texas breakfast with a European flair. Escape from the hectic world is easy on The Castle Inn's six acres of park-like grounds.

Historical Significance:

This Recorded Texas Historic Landmark home was built in 1893 by Ward Templeman — merchant, cotton dealer, and oil investor — for his bride, Annie Foster Templeman. Originally a Queen Anne design, it was crafted to make extensive use of now-extinct curly pine, beveled glass, intricate inlaid flooring, and ornate brasswork. The house was bricked and modified in the early 20th century to reflect elements of the Prairie style of architecture.

Places To Go, Sites To See:

Historic Navasota is a town with beautiful turn-of-the-century homes, parks, and antique shops. The downtown area is listed in the National Register of Historic Places. The Castle Inn is only ten minutes from Washington-on-the-Brazos State Historical Park, and twenty-five minutes from Bryan/College Station, home of Texas A&M University and the George Bush Memorial Library.

Historic Kuebler-Waldrip Haus and Danville School

1620 Hueco Springs Loop Road
New Braunfels, TX 78132-3001

800-299-8372
830-625-8372
E-mail: kwb&b@compuvision.net
Website:
www.nbtexas.com/kueblerwaldrip

Hosts: Margaret K. Waldrip and
son, Darrell Waldrip

BEDS: 10 rooms, 10 private baths

BREAKFAST & OTHER MEALS: Full breakfast

$$, $$$ Open all year, two night minimum on weekends, three night minimum on holiday weekends

Relax in a beautifully restored hand-hewn limestone and log pioneer home or an original one-room schoolhouse on a 43-acre Texas Hill Country ranch. The comfortable rooms all have private baths (two are wheelchair accessible; four have whirlpools), TVs, VCRs, and phones; some have kitchens. Winter evenings may be spent by the fireplace. Enjoy an elegantly served breakfast with specialty cinnamon rolls, or possibly with a Spanish flair since Margaret is a certified Spanish teacher. Spanish lessons and Mexico tours are available, as well as shopping in the gift shop which features lovely Mexican imported items. Enjoy a peaceful country setting, Texas wildlife and warm hospitality.

Historical Significance:

The land was once owned by Francois Guilbeau, a French-born wine merchant credited with saving the blighted French vineyards with mustang grape cuttings from this property. The 1847 home, built by Andreas Pape of Germany, was restored by the Waldrips and sons, Dibrell, Darrell, and David. The 1863 Danville School (Comal County) was bought at auction in 1990, moved and restored, making a perfect facility for business retreats, weddings, and family reunions.

Places To Go, Sites To See:

This spacious ranch is just minutes from a huge number of attractions, river recreation, fine dining, and shopping in the New Braunfels/Gruene area.

Karbach Haus Bed and Breakfast Home

487 West San Antonio Street
New Braunfels, TX 78130

800-972-5941
830-625-2131
Fax: 830-629-1126
E-mail: khausbnb@aol.com

Hosts: Captain Ben Jack Kinney, USN (Ret) and Kathy Karbach Kinney, PhD

BEDS: 5 rooms, 1 suite, 6 private baths

BREAKFAST & OTHER MEALS: Full gourmet breakfast

$$$ Open all year, two night minimum for Saturday night stays, three night minimum over holiday weekends

In this traditional B&B setting, guests experience the Gemütlichkeit of a German Gästehaus with the amenities of a romantic, upscale resort. Stately and casually elegant, the home boasts turn-of-the-century ambiance with twentieth-century comforts. Each spacious guest room has a private tile bath, queen or king-size bed, cable TV/VCR, ceiling fan, and many antiques and family heirlooms. A luxury suite above the carriage house includes a full kitchen and private entrance. The 18x40 swimming pool and spa are set in beautifully landscaped gardens, surrounded by ancient pecan, cypress and magnolia trees. A German-style, multi-course breakfast is graciously served each morning in the sun parlor or formal dining room.

Historical Significance:

Kathy's parents purchased this stately turn-of-the-century mansion in the mid-thirties. Extensive remodeling rendered it the most modern residence in town, perfect for the prominent doctor's large family and a Mecca for the city's elite. Kathy and Ben Jack married at the home in 1956.

Places To Go, Sites To See:

Conveniently located on an acre estate in the heart of downtown New Braunfels, visitors may walk to a superb variety of restaurants, museums, and antique stores. Picnic in Landa Park, thrill to Schlitterbahn, browse in Gruene Historic District, or enjoy tubing or river-rafting.

The Old Hunter Road
Stagecoach Inn B&B

5441 FM 1102
New Braunfels, TX 78132

800-201-2912
830-620-9453

Host: Bettina Messinger

BEDS: 3 rooms, 3 private baths

BREAKFAST & OTHER MEALS: Full breakfast

$, $$ Open all year, two night minimum on weekends

Step into another era of Texas history as you enter the 1848 hand-hewn LogPen Cabin or the German Fachwerk house built in 1850. Lovingly restored, this historic inn features cedar-beamed rooms furnished with a wealth of early Texas antiques including enormous walnut and cedar beds, old rockers, and period paintings. Each guest room has a private bath with a claw foot or tin tub. Restoration is underway to add two more accommodations, which will include a hot tub and will be handicap accessible. Bettina, a landscape designer, has surrounded the homes with native plants, fragrant herbs, and antique roses. She serves a gourmet breakfast which may include her specialty, Swedish pancakes.

Historical Significance:

The Old Hunter Road Stagecoach Inn was built in 1850 as a stagecoach stop between New Braunfels and San Marcos. Some of the pens used for boarding the horses can still be seen. The cabins are hand-hewn logs, the house is hand-hewn Fachwerk construction.

Places To Go, Sites To See:

The Inn is less than five minutes from Gruene and all the arts and crafts studios, boutique shops, eating establishments, and water activities. Gruene Hall, the oldest continuously operating dance hall in Texas, still features name performers such as Jerry Jeff Walker and Willie Nelson.

Prince Solms Inn

295 E. San Antonio Street
New Braunfels, TX 78130

800-625-9169
830-625-9169

Host: Deborah Redle

BEDS: 10 rooms/suites, 10 private baths

BREAKFAST & OTHER MEALS: Continental Plus breakfast; restaurant on premises

$, $$, $$$ Open all year

The Prince Solms Inn is centrally located near the Main Plaza, a block from the clear Comal, the world's shortest river. Elegantly furnished with European antiques and artwork, the Inn has a gentile, refined Old World atmosphere. Its German heritage is evident in thick brick walls, Victorian detailing, and the impressive ten-foot front doors with intricately etched glass panels. Behind the Inn, a picturesque, brick courtyard laden with lush plants and flowers, offers a shady spot to relax. Wolfgang's Keller, named in honor of composer Wolfgang Mozart, is a restaurant and bar located in the cellar, serving excellent Continental cuisine in romantic surroundings.

Historical Significance:

A Recorded Texas Historic Landmark, the Prince Solms Inn has been in continuous operation since it was built by German craftsmen in 1898. The soft beige bricks, handmade for the hotel, were carted to the construction site by horse-drawn wagons. The Cypress was milled from giant trees on the banks of the Guadalupe River.

Places To Go, Sites To See:

New Braunfels offers an endless variety of attractions and activities: tubing on Comal River, Landa Park and golf course, Schlitterbahn Waterpark, Hummel Museum, Natural Bridge Caverns, Outlet Shopping Mall, and the historic downtown area with its antique shops and restaurants.

Moonlight Bay
B&B

506 South Bay Blvd.
Palacios, TX 77465

800-714-1997 (code: 51)
512-972-2232
E-mail: grogers@bayareacom.net

Hosts: Earl and Gaye Rogers-Hudson

BEDS: 7 rooms, 7 private baths

BREAKFAST & OTHER MEALS: Full breakfast; luncheons and dinners for a minimum of eight are available with advance reservations

$$, $$$ Open all year

On Fridays and Saturdays at 4:00 p.m., your hostess plays music from the 1940s on the grand piano while tea is served in the parlor. Thus begins your transition to quiet elegance. Four romantic, upstairs guest rooms have names like Moonlight & Roses and Stardust. Two in front share a spacious, enclosed balcony overlooking the bay. The house, featuring a dark green and burgundy color scheme, is restored to the grand lady she was in 1910 and retains many original fixtures and leaded glass. As you enjoy the spectacular views of the bay from garden verandas, you can almost hear the music of Harry James from the landmark Pavilion bandstand across the way. Three additional accommodations are available at "Paper Moon," a 1930s house next door which Gaye has cleverly decorated with a literary theme. Every wall showcases extraordinary original murals by artist Roberta St. Paul.

Historical Significance:

This 1910 waterfront home was alive with parties for the officers at Camp Hulen during WW II. The Frank Lloyd Wright Prairie style structure was one of the first homes in Palacios. Your hostess is the fourth owner and has created a new era of hospitality for her guests.

Places To Go, Sites To See:

This peaceful, "undiscovered" city by the bay has sailing regattas, fishing from lighted piers, golf, a lighted seawall walkway, and 218 species of birds. It was headquarters for the excavation of the 300-year-old shipwreck "LaBelle," and the home of the Texas State Marine Education Center.

The Carson House Inn & Grille

302 Mt. Pleasant Street
Pittsburg, TX 75686

888-302-1878
903-856-2468
Fax: 903-856-0709
E-Mail:carsonig@1starnet.com

Hosts: Eileen and Clark
Jesmore

BEDS: 4 rooms, 1 suite, 3 private baths, 1 shared bath

BREAKFAST & OTHER MEALS: Continental breakfast (Full breakfast available for $5/per person extra); full service restaurant on premises

$, $$ Open all year

The Carson House Inn showcases some stunning examples of curly pine wainscoting and wood trim from the now-extinct curly pine tree originally found in Louisiana. Furnished with turn-of-the-century antiques, each guest room and suite has cable TV, a coffee maker, and gourmet teas; complimentary soft drinks are available in the restaurant. One room, in a converted rail car behind the house, is decorated with railroad memorabilia and offers complete privacy. A Jacuzzi on the deck is for all guests. The ambiance is favorable for romantic weekends, and yet the inn is suitably equipped for business travelers as well. The upscale restaurant offers fine dining, featuring excellent selections of steaks, seafood, chicken, salad, sandwiches, and pasta dishes. A full bar is available. Smoking is allowed in the restaurant only. The first floor restaurant is also wheelchair accessible.

Historical Significance:

Built in 1878 and fully restored 111 years later, the Carson House is the oldest home in Pittsburg. It remains in its original location, and features an exceptionally large quantity of rare curly pine woodwork.

Places To Go, Sites To See:

An official Main Street City, Pittsburg has a variety of interesting shops in its restored downtown area. Centrally located in East Texas, it is near several golf courses, great fishing and recreation lakes, state parks, and innumerable antique shops. Pittsburg is also home to the Ezekiel airship.

Hoopes' House

417 North Broadway
Rockport, TX 78382

800-924-1008
512-729-8424
Fax: 512-790-9288

Host: Laura Casterline, Mgr.

BEDS: 8 rooms, 8 private baths

BREAKFAST & OTHER MEALS: Full breakfast

$$$ Open all year, minimum stay requirements on some holidays

Hoopes' House, an elegant 2½ story Queen Anne Victorian home, has a panoramic view of Rockport's harbor and overlooks the beach. The bay-windowed reception room, with its inviting fireplace and carved mantel, welcomes you to an earlier era. Meticulously restored to its original grandeur, this stunning home features "Four Seasons" stained-glass windows, pocket doors and broad pine floors. Lavishly decorated in the Victorian style, the spacious rooms are furnished with many antiques original to the house. Four guest rooms are upstairs and four new "garden rooms" have been recently built on the grounds. All guest rooms have private baths with robes and fine toiletries, telephones, and cable television. A swimming pool, hot tub, and gazebo offer relaxation amid the manicured lawn and gardens behind the home.

Historical Significance:

Listed in the National Register of Historic Places, this prominent landmark was built between 1890-1892 by J.M. Hoopes, a local banker and land developer. Over the years, it has been both a private residence and a luxury hotel.

Places To Go, Sites To See:

Hoopes' House is in the heart of Rockport's historic downtown, within walking distance of museums, art galleries, and unique shopping boutiques. Rockport, with its world-renowned bird watching and great fishing, is located on Aransas Bay, just 30 minutes from Padre Island and Corpus Christi.

Heart of My Heart Ranch

403 Florida Chapel Road
P.O. Box 106
Round Top, TX 78954

800-327-1242
Fax: 409-249-3171
E-Mail: heart17@cvtv.net
Website: www.virtualcities.com/
ons/tx/a/txa7601.htm

Hosts: Frances and Bill Harris

BEDS: 13 rooms and suites, 13 private baths

BREAKFAST & OTHER MEALS: Full breakfast; other meals for groups by arrangement

$$$ Open all year, two night minimum on weekends

Frances and Bill converted their ranch to this antique-filled Historic Inn and Conference Center in 1990. Over the years, Heart of My Heart Ranch has grown to six buildings, including two two-bedroom units, all with private baths and covered porches. A fishing lake, island, boats, and pier were added first. Next came a swimming pool, hot tub, and Swedish massage. Then a game room, horses, hiking trails, bicycles, in-room color television and VCR, and a video library. Now it is both a secluded, romantic getaway and a family resort, perfect for meetings and retreats. Visitors on Monday nights enjoy a cookout at the ranch.

Historical Significance:

The 1836 log cabin was the birthplace of Joel Robinson, the hero who captured Santa Anna at San Jacinto. A larger log home is that of Jared Gross, the father of Texas agriculture. Gaucher Trace, the first road in Texas, crosses the ranch.

Places To Go, Sites To See:

Round Top, population 81, is one of the most appealing towns in Texas. The restored "museum village," Henkel Square, demonstrates 19th century cultures. Winedale Historic Center is a center for the study of ethnic cultures of central Texas. The internationally acclaimed Festival Hill Institute of Classical Music gives concerts most of the year. Bethlehem Lutheran Church houses a native cedar pipe organ built in 1867.

The Settlement at Round Top

2218 Hartfield Road
P.O. Box 176
Round Top, TX 78954

888-RoundTop
409-249-5015
E-mail: setlment@cvtv.net

Hosts: Karen and Larry Beevers

BEDS: 8 rooms, 8 private baths

BREAKFAST & OTHER MEALS: Full breakfast on weekends, Continental breakfast on weekdays; picnic lunches or dinners available with advance notice

$$, $$$ Open all year, two night minimum for selected cabins on weekends, additional restrictions during special events

Featured in the June 1997 issue of *Country Living* magazine, The Settlement at Round Top is an interesting cluster of curiously diverse restored nineteenth-century buildings surrounded by thirty-five scenic acres of wildflowers, ponds, split rail fences, deer, miniature horses, and massive oak trees. All accommodations, from an old Santa Fe Railroad ticket office to a general store to a dog trot and a two-story log cabin, are beautifully decorated and feature private baths, central heat/air, and porches; some have fireplaces or whirlpool tubs for two. Choose a different building each time you visit. Karen and Larry have also restored an enormous barn to accommodate conventions, weddings, and family reunions.

Historical Significance:

Confederate soldiers helped raise the main house while a family of eight lived in a primitive one-room log cabin. The cabin walls still stand behind the restored home where your hosts now live. The cedar cottage (Das Kleine Nest) and the Barn were part of the original 1860's homestead. The rest of the buildings were moved from nearby sites and carefully restored by Karen and Larry.

Places To Go, Sites To See:

The tiny German community of Round Top, population 81, hosts one of the largest antique shows in the U.S. each April and October. Up to 100,000 people invade the area looking for special treasures. Home of renowned pianist, James Dick, Festival Hill Institute features outstanding concerts. Spectacular springtime wildflower shows abound in the surrounding countryside.

The Rose Mansion

1 Rose Way
Salado, TX 76571

800-948-1004
254-947-8200
Website:
www.touringtexas.
  com/rose

Hosts: Neil and Carole
  Hunter

BEDS: 10 rooms, 10 private baths

BREAKFAST & OTHER MEALS: Full breakfast

$$, $$$ Open all year

Nestled among towering oak, elm, and persimmon trees, this Greek Revival style mansion is situated on two acres of beautifully landscaped grounds surrounded by a white picket fence. Recently featured in *Southern Living*, the Mansion is furnished with authentic antiques and Rose family heirlooms and memorabilia. Four guest rooms are in the main house, others are in picturesque restored log cabins and cottages on the property. All accommodations have queen-sized beds and several have fireplaces. A gourmet breakfast is served in the Mansion's dining room. Shaded seating areas, swings, and hammocks are everywhere, inviting relaxation and tranquility.

Historical Significance:

The grounds offer a mini-tour of early Texas dwellings. Listed in the National Register of Historic Places, the property also proudly displays two Recorded Texas Historic Landmark plaques attesting to the authenticity of the Rose Mansion, built in 1870 by Major A.J. Rose, as well as two restored log cabins, an original kitchen cottage, and a Greek Revival cottage.

Places To Go, Sites To See:

Stroll through the quaint village of Salado for fine antiques, clothing, and unique gifts. Golf, tennis, swimming, and carriage rides are available nearby. Excellent restaurants in historic buildings offer a variety of cuisine.

Inn at Salado

307 North Main Street
Salado, TX 76571

800-724-0027
254-947-0027
Website:
www.lone-star.net/
innatsalado

Host: Suzanne Petro

BEDS: 9 rooms, 9 private baths

BREAKFAST & OTHER MEALS: Full breakfast; catering available

$, $$, $$$ Open all year, two night minimum on some weekends

A Recorded Texas Historic Landmark, Salado's first Bed & Breakfast is located in the heart of the historic district of this charming village. The interior is furnished throughout with lovely antiques, and most guest rooms have king or queen-sized beds and fireplaces. Six covered porches with swings and two tree-shaded brick terraces encourage relaxation and people-watching. Wander around the two landscaped acres framed with white picket fencing, and see the original hand-dug well. A homemade gourmet breakfast is served buffet style in the formal dining room.

Historical Significance:

Listed in the National Register of Historic Places, the Inn was built in 1872 and exhibits classical and Victorian detailing. One of the first owners, Colonel James Norton, was a prominent local citizen and donated granite from his rock quarry to be used in the construction of the State Capitol. In the past, the building was used as a boarding house for travelers and teachers at Salado College.

Places To Go, Sites To See:

Located on Main Street, Inn at Salado is steps from the interesting variety of shops, boutiques, galleries, and restaurants. Mill Creek Golf Course is nearby and the area is pleasant for bicycling, jogging, or walking.

Academy House of Monte Vista

2317 N. Main Avenue
San Antonio, TX 78212-3448

888-731-8393
210-731-8393
Fax: 210-431-3953 attn: Johnnie
                          Walker-Staggs
E-Mail: academyh@netxpress.com
Website: www.netxpress.com/academyh

Hosts: Kenneth and Johnnie Walker-Staggs

BEDS: 3 rooms, 3 private baths

BREAKFAST & OTHER MEALS: Full breakfast

$$, $$$ Open all year, two night minimum on weekends

The Academy House is an unpretentious 1897 two-story white frame Victorian across from San Antonio Academy and close to Trinity University. Shaded by giant pecan trees, it offers the peace and quiet of the century-old Monte Vista historic neighborhood while only minutes from downtown. The home is comfortably furnished with antiques and richly appointed in shades of raspberry, wine, and antique white. Each guest bedroom has its own character featuring deep plum carpet and a comfortable king-size bed, as well as the modern conveniences of cable television and telephone. The honeymoon cottage features a Jacuzzi tub for two. A delicious breakfast is served in the formal dining room by the gregarious and interesting hosts.

Historical Significance:

The Academy House was built in 1897 by attorney John Hiram Clark. In 1914, it was purchased by Frost Woodhull, of the financially and socially prominent Frost and Woodhull families. In 1937, Virginia Berry, founder of La Fonda restaurant, purchased the home which remained in her family until 1994 when the Staggs purchased it to restore as a Bed & Breakfast.

Places To Go, Sites To See:

The Riverwalk, Alamo, Market Square, Mission Trail, Brackenridge Park, Fiesta Texas, and Sea World are popular San Antonio attractions.

A Yellow Rose
Bed & Breakfast

229 Madison
San Antonio, TX 78204

800-950-9903
210-229-9903
Fax: 210-229-1691
E-Mail: yellowrs@express-news.net

Hosts: Deb Field-Walker & Kit Walker

BEDS: 5 rooms, 5 private baths

BREAKFAST & OTHER MEALS: Full breakfast

$$, $$$ Open all year, two night minimum on weekends and holidays

A Yellow Rose Bed & Breakfast is an elegant Victorian home in the quiet, residential King William Historic District. Numerous original features have been preserved, including the triple hung, stenciled glass window in the entry. Five spacious guest rooms are tastefully decorated with antiques; each has central heat and air, ceiling fan, queen-size bed, cable TV, clock alarm, radio, and a private, modern bathroom. Guests are encouraged to enjoy the spacious parlor which is separated from the grand empire dining room by massive 10-foot red pine pocket doors. Both rooms are furnished with lovely turn-of-the-century antiques. A full gourmet breakfast is served in the formal dining room each morning. Make plans for the day's activities while relaxing on one of the large porches — your enthusiastic hosts can offer recommendations, maps, and brochures. Off-street, covered parking is provided.

Historical Significance:

This splendid residence boasts exemplary craftsmanship, both inside and out. Built in two stages, it presents a fascinating contrast in styles and building materials. Now attached, the original Sunday house portion was built around 1865 and the main house was built in 1878 by Charles Mueller.

Places To Go, Sites To See:

A Yellow Rose is conveniently located two blocks from the serene, residential part of the Riverwalk, one block from the 50-cent trolley, five blocks from downtown and within three blocks of some of the finest restaurants in San Antonio.

Brackenridge House "a bed and breakfast inn"

230 Madison
San Antonio, TX 78204

800-221-1412
210-271-3442
Fax: 210-226-3139
E-Mail: benniesueb@aol.com
Website: www.brackenridgehouse.com

Hosts: Bennie and Sue Blansett

BEDS: 3 rooms, 2 suites, 5 private baths

BREAKFAST & OTHER MEALS: Full breakfast

$$, $$$ Open all year, two night minimum on weekends and holidays

The Brackenridge House, inspected and rated excellent by AAA, Mobil, and American Bed and Breakfast Association, offers excellent accommodations for visitors to San Antonio. In the words of Bennie and Sue, their Inn is "owner occupied (we live here) and managed (we do all the work)." The home features original pine floors, high ceilings, and lovely antique furnishings. Three guest rooms and two suites provide queen or king-size beds, cable television (HBO and ShowTime), mini-refrigerators, coffee makers, telephones, and private baths. Guests may relax on the front porch, or in the rear patio garden area with its large hot tub, swings, and rockers. Sue's breakfast is a formally served gourmet delight.

Historical Significance:

Built in 1901 by John Brackenridge, this beautiful Greek Revival home has stood the test of time; not only changing owners several times but also from family home to apartments to B&B. In 1986, Carolyn Cole, the former owner, received a Conservation Society award for her outstanding restoration.

Places To Go, Sites To See:

Located in the King William Historic District, the Brackenridge House is a five-minute trolley ride from all the nearby attractions of downtown San Antonio. Numerous restaurants and shops are nearby.

The Columns on Alamo

1037 S. Alamo
San Antonio, TX 78210

800-233-3364
210-271-3245
Fax: 210-271-3245
Website:
www.thecolumnsbandbinn.com

Hosts: Ellenor and Arthur Link

BEDS: 11 rooms, 11 private baths

BREAKFAST & OTHER MEALS: Full breakfast

$$, $$$ Open all year, two night minimum on weekends

The AAA four-diamond rated Columns on Alamo was established in 1994 by innkeepers Ellenor and Art Link in their gracious 1892 Greek Revival home and the adjacent 1901 Guest House. The Columns offers off-street parking and over an acre of landscaped grounds. Choose from eleven guest rooms with queen or king-size beds, comfortable Victorian antique furnishings, verandas, private baths, televisions and telephones, fireplaces, and Jacuzzis. Relax on the porches or in the common areas before or after a busy day. Breakfast is served in the main house each morning. Ellenor and Art are available to suggest excursion itineraries, dining and shopping adventures, and cultural and seasonal events unique to San Antonio.

Historical Significance:

The Columns on Alamo is located in the King William Historic District which features an exceptional variety of palatial mansions as well as small historic homes from the late 1800s. Take the self-guided walking tour or the guided home tour to experience the history of this area.

Places To Go, Sites To See:

Take the antique trolley, which stops in front of The Columns, to all the major attractions of downtown San Antonio. It's only a few minutes' drive to Seaworld or Fiesta Texas, award- winning golf courses, and the Spanish missions.

The Fairmount Hotel

401 South Alamo Street
San Antonio, TX 78205

800-642-3363
210-224-8800
Fax: 210-224-2767

Host: Les Utley, Gen. Mgr.

BEDS: 20 rooms, 17 suites, 37 private baths

BREAKFAST & OTHER MEALS: Some included with special packages; restaurant on premises

$$$ Open all year

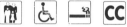

The Fairmount Hotel, located in the heart of historic downtown San Antonio, is one of the finest small luxury hotels in the country. Enter a world of casual elegance and southwestern comfort… a world of high ceilings, fine stone and marble, rich natural wood, soft colors, chandeliers, fine art, fresh flowers. Furnished with individual decor, guest rooms and suites feature canopied beds, overstuffed chairs, imported marble baths, full-length terry robes, and plush, oversized towels. Suites afford the finest amenities, entertainment centers with television and VCR, and exquisite art. Guests may dine in the lush garden courtyard or visit the four diamond award-winning Polo's Restaurant which offers casual elegance and fine food. Catering to travelers, from honeymooners to international business executives, the Fairmount staff offers exceptional personal service.

Historical Significance:

Built in 1906, The Fairmount has details of the Italiante Victorian style. It made history (and the Guiness Book of World Records) when it was moved six blocks through the streets of San Antonio to its present location in 1985. Moving the 3.2 million-pound, 42-foot tall building took six days and involved turning two corners and crossing the Riverwalk on a specially reinforced bridge.

Places To Go, Sites To See:

The Fairmount is steps from the exciting Riverwalk and La Villita Marketplace. Centrally located in downtown San Antonio, The Fairmount is convenient for business or pleasure travelers.

Noble Inns

107 Madison and 102 Turner St.
San Antonio, TX 78204

800-221-4045
210-225-4045
Fax: 210-227-0877
E-mail: nobleinns@aol.com
Website: www.nobleinns.com

Hosts: Donald and Liesl Noble

BEDS: 6 rooms, 3 suites, 9 private baths

BREAKFAST & OTHER MEALS: Full or Continental Plus breakfast

$$$ Open all year

Noble Inns consists of two Victorian-era properties which have been meticulously restored and decorated with fine antiques, designer decor, and luxurious amenities. Each accommodation features a fireplace with antique mantel, color cable TV with HBO, telephone with voice mail and data port, and marble bath with two-person Jacuzzi or claw foot tub. Find privacy in Pancoast Carriage House's spacious suites with kitchens and continental breakfasts. Guests may enjoy an outdoor pool and heated spa in the garden/patio area. The traditional Jackson House B&B offers breakfasts served in the dining room. Its garden offers a heated swim spa in a stained glass conservatory. Life-long San Antonians and descendants of original King William founding families, the Nobles have created settings that reflect taste and gracious elegance.

Historical Significance:

Both properties are located in San Antonio's King William Historic District and designated as historic landmarks. The two-story Pancoast Carriage House stands behind the owner's residence, built in 1896 for Don's great-grandfather. The Jackson House is a two-story brick and limestone home constructed in 1894.

Places To Go, Sites To See:

Noble Inns properties are a short walk from the Alamo and Riverwalk, and steps from the trolley that will take you around downtown. Spanish Missions, Fiesta Texas and Seaworld are nearby.

The Royal Swan

236 Madison Street
San Antonio, TX 78204

800-368-3073
210-223-3776
Fax: 210-271-0373
E-Mail: theswan@onr.com
Website: www.royalswan.com

Hosts: Curt and Helen Skredergard

BEDS: 4 rooms, 1 suite, 5 private baths

BREAKFAST & OTHER MEALS: Full breakfast

$$, $$$ Open all year, two night minimum on weekends, holidays, and during some special events

Curt and Helen enjoy sharing their splendid Victorian home in the King William Historic District of San Antonio. Guests immediately feel welcome as they step into the original, native Texas long-leaf pine entry foyer with its grand staircase. Warmth radiates from the patina of old, well-cared-for wood. This fine home is a showcase for other original features such as magnificent stained-glass windows and two downstairs fireplaces. The Royal Swan is elegantly furnished throughout with period antiques. Each spacious guest room has a queen-size bed, cable television, telephone, and coffee maker. A savory breakfast is served in the sunny morning room or the formal dining room. Complimentary sodas and home-baked goodies are always available.

Historical Significance:

Built in 1892 by Dr. Jabez Cain in what was to become the King William Historic District, this grand Victorian remains essentially unchanged. The original carriage curbstone bearing Dr. Cain's name can still be found in front of the house.

Places To Go, Sites To See:

Conveniently located two blocks from the Riverwalk and six blocks from downtown, the Royal Swan is just steps from the trolley which conveys visitors to the major attractions, museums, shopping, and sights of San Antonio.

Crystal River Inn

326 W. Hopkins
San Marcos, TX 78666

888-396-3739
512-396-3739
Fax: 512-353-3248

Hosts: Cathy, Mike, and Sarah Dillon

BEDS: 13 rooms and suites, 11 private baths, 1 shared bath

BREAKFAST & OTHER MEALS: Full breakfast; Catered luncheons, dinners, parties, and weddings available

$$, $$$ Open all year, two night minimum most weekends

The Crystal River Inn with its designer-appointed rooms has been featured in numerous magazines such as *Southern Living* and *Country Inns* and has earned a three-star rating by Mobil Travel Guide. Guest accommodations are in three buildings; the Main House and the Rock House are separated by carefully tended gardens with roses, topiaries, fountains, and towering pecan trees. Fireplaces, canopied beds, TVs, phones, and sitting rooms contribute to guests' comfort. Full gourmet breakfasts are headliner events — Eggs Benedict, Bananas Foster crepes, and Raspberry French toast. The Dillons can arrange for carriage rides, European massages, and are widely renowned for their theme weekends: romance getaways, adventure river trips, "for ladies only," and especially their murder mystery weekends which focus on real people and events in San Marcos history.

Historical Significance:

San Marcos' founding father, Judge W. O. Wood, built this grand home in 1883. It was the town's first Victorian house. The architectural style was changed to Greek Revival in 1906, with the addition of verandas and Corinthian columns.

Places To Go, Sites To See:

San Marcos' most outstanding tourist attributes are its crystal clear river (tube it, canoe it, or take a glass-bottom boat cruise at Aquarena Springs); its three splendid historic districts, and the huge designer outlet mall with 150 stores.

The Pelican House

1302 1st Street
Seabrook, TX 77586
281-474-5295
Host: Suzanne Silver

BEDS: 4 rooms, 4 private baths

BREAKFAST & OTHER MEALS: Full breakfast

$$ Open all year, no restrictions

The Pelican House is a turn-of-the-century "Grandma's House" with a whimsical twist. Suzanne had fun decorating this cottage with a beach theme of pelicans, seashells, and fish using faux paintings, murals, and stencils. Each guest room has a private bath and queen-size bed, two have great views of the water and one has French doors that open onto the back deck. Pecan and live oak trees are plentiful on the landscaped grounds, and the property slopes gently to meet the back bay. A front porch with rockers is inviting, and the back deck is a haven for water bird viewing at its best. For a special treat, plan your visit between October and March when hundreds of pelicans stay in the bay within yards of the house. Suzanne does not live on-site, but will meet guests on arrival and reappear each morning to cook and serve a delicious breakfast.

Historical Significance:

Built in 1906 as a family home, it housed one of Seabrook's first school teachers. The house has survived three major hurricanes.

Places To Go, Sites To See:

Located in the Seabrook arts and antiques colony, the Pelican House is within walking distance of several interesting shops, art galleries, and restaurants, and is the closest bed & breakfast to Space Center Houston.

Weinert House

1207 N. Austin St.
Seguin, TX 78155

888-303-0912
830-372-0422
Fax: 830-303-0912

Hosts: Lynna and Tom
Thomas

BEDS: 3 rooms, 1 suite, 4 private baths

BREAKFAST & OTHER MEALS: Full breakfast; dinners, luncheons, and picnics with advance notice

$$, $$$ Open all year, two night minimum on holidays

The elegant Weinert House is one of Seguin's premiere Victorian homes. Built in 1895 by Texas Senator and Secretary of State, F.C. Weinert, the home displays an outstanding collection of original furnishings, fixtures, and heirlooms of Senator Weinert and his family. The parlor and music room feature splendid, original hand-painted friezes. Four upstairs guest rooms have king or queen-size beds, elegant antique furnishings, and private baths; three have fireplaces, one has a screened sun porch. Lynna lives nearby but welcomes guests upon arrival and serves formal, gourmet breakfasts. Small business conferences can be accommodated in the dining room. A glassed sunroom easily accommodates 35 and is perfect for luncheons, teas, and parties.

Historical Significance:

Built in 1895 on farmland, the Weinert House has its original outbuildings – a carriage house/barn and smokehouse. A true Queen Anne Victorian, the house has been featured in *Texas Highways* magazine and the Society of Architectural Historians publications.

Places To Go, Sites To See:

Seguin's location gives guests access to its historic treasures, as well as the attractions of nearby San Antonio, New Braunfels, Gruene, and San Marcos. The best-selling novel, *TRUE WOMEN*, was set in this area, and both self-guided and group *TRUE WOMEN* tours are currently popular.

The Katy House

201 Ramona
Smithville, TX 78957

800-The-Katy (843-5289)
512-237-4262
E-Mail: thekatyh@onr.com
Website:
www.katyhouse.com

Hosts: Bruce and Sallie
Blalock

BEDS: 4 rooms, 4 private baths

BREAKFAST & OTHER MEALS: Full breakfast

$, $$ Open all year

This Recorded Texas Historic Landmark 1909 home, furnished with American period antiques and filled with railroad memorabilia, reflects the spirit and heritage of Central Texas. Graceful columns, high ceilings, and detailed millwork along with original longleaf pine floors, pocket doors and leaded and beveled glass detail the home. The ambiance is one of gracious comfort. All rooms have private baths with original claw foot tubs, televisions, and telephones. Antique beds have been converted to queen-size. Separate from the main house, the Carriage House features Western decor, and the Conductors' Quarters feature a railroad theme. Sallie serves a bountiful breakfast feast in the dining room.

Historical Significance:

Named for the "Katy" (Missouri Kansas & Texas) Railroad with local headquarters in Smithville, and built by a successful area businessman, the home remains virtually original. The second owner, Dr. J.D. Stephens, a railroad division surgeon, established his practice in the parlor. Bruce and Sallie's family roots are here too, with Smithville and with the railroad.

Places To Go, Sites To See:

A city of beautiful old neighborhoods with tree-lined streets, the Smithville area has everything from recreation to relaxation, antiquing, sightseeing, and dining.

McLachlan Farm Bed & Breakfast

24907 Hardy
P.O. Box 538
Spring, TX 77383

800-382-3988
281-350-2400
Fax: 281-288-1011

Hosts: Jim and Joycelyn
Clairmonte

BEDS: 3 or 4 rooms, 3 private baths

BREAKFAST & OTHER MEALS: Full breakfast

$$, $$$ Open all year

The short drive down a shady, gravel lane leads to a secluded yellow and white farmhouse nestled among towering pecan trees on 35 acres of neatly mowed lawns and winding forest trails. A sincere Southern welcome awaits inside, if the swings on the wrap-around porches don't entice you first. Guest rooms are comfortably furnished with family antiques, quilts, and heirlooms. Bathrooms provide plush towels and bubble bath for those long soaks in claw foot tubs. A cozy family room with a fireplace is for visiting, porches are for relaxing. You won't leave hungry after Joy's ample breakfast specialties such as pumpkin-nut French toast, pineapple ham quiche, or Swedish pancakes.

Historical Significance:

The McLachlan family settled this land in 1861. Joy's grandfather, Charles McLachlan, built the farmhouse for his family in 1911. He farmed, worked on the railroad, and served as superintendent of Spring schools for seventeen years. Joy is the fourth generation to live on the land. Her husband, Jim, enlarged the house in 1989 and they opened it to B&B guests in 1990.

Places To Go, Sites To See:

This farming and railroad community was founded in the mid-1800s. Now Old Town Spring is a quaint shopping village with over 150 antique, gift, and craft shops located one mile north of McLachlan Farm and 20 miles north of Houston.

The Oxford House

563 N. Graham
Stephenville, TX 76401

800-711-7283
254-965-6885

Host: Paula Oxford

BEDS: 4 rooms, 4 private baths

BREAKFAST & OTHER MEALS: Full breakfast; candlelight dinners and English teas by reservation only

$$ Open all year

The Oxford house is a beautifully restored Queen Anne Victorian home constructed in 1898. Pale blue with dark blue and burgundy trim, the house has four upstairs guest rooms with private baths, specialty soaps and claw foot tubs for long soaks. An 1890s sleigh bed, marble top dressers, and antique armoires enhance the Victorian charm of the bedrooms. During her restoration research, Paula became fascinated with the Oxford family history and has displayed portraits, heirlooms and memorabilia throughout the home. Paula and her family live nearby, and she will serve a gourmet breakfast each morning. Spacious porches, complete with rocking chairs, surround the home. A garden area with gazebo and fountains has been the setting for numerous weddings.

Historical Significance:

Shortly before becoming a judge, attorney W.J. Oxford, Sr. collected $3000 in silver coins as a fee for a lawsuit. He used the funds to finance this picturesque Stephenville landmark, which, true to the Victorian style, has abundant hand-turned gingerbread trim, spacious porches, and a cupola.

Places To Go, Sites To See:

Stephenville is the home of Tarleton State University. The Stephenville Country Opry (Branson style) offers entertainment. Nearby Glen Rose offers several attractions.

Rosevine Inn Bed & Breakfast

415 S. Vine
Tyler, TX 75702

903-592-2221
E-Mail:
rosevine@iamerica.net

Hosts: Bert and Becca
Powell

BEDS: 5 rooms, 2 suites, 7 private baths

BREAKFAST & OTHER MEALS: Full breakfast

$$, $$$ Open all year except Christmas Eve and Christmas Day

Tyler's first Bed & Breakfast is built on the foundation where a large English Tudor mansion once stood and mysteriously burned to the ground in 1969. Rosevine Inn was built to recreate the look and feel of a vintage 1930s home but with modern conveniences, including insulation in all interior walls between guest rooms. The living area features a 1928 Aeolian Player Piano and furnishings from the '20s and '30s. Guest accommodations are in the main house, a circa 1934 brick cottage, and the Lodge Room. The Lodge Room is above the gameroom which has a rock fireplace, billiard table, ping-pong table, and other games. There are outdoor fireplaces, a courtyard with fountain, and a hot tub. A formal breakfast is served in the dining room of the main house.

Historical Significance:

Rosevine Inn is located in the historic Brick Street District of Tyler, in the Pope Place addition which was the original homestead of Dr. Irvin Pope, one of the city's first physicians. A circa 1934 brick cottage, behind the Inn, has been restored to near-original condition.

Places To Go, Sites To See:

Tyler is know as the Rose Capital of America. The main attractions include the grand municipal rose garden, rose museum and gift shop, antique shops and museums.

The Seasons Bed & Breakfast Inn

313 E. Charnwood
Tyler, TX 75701

903-533-0803

Hosts: Jim and Myra
Brown

BEDS: 4 rooms, 4 private baths

BREAKFAST & OTHER MEALS: Full breakfast; picnic baskets available

$$, $$$ Open all year except Christmas Day

This Southern Colonial style mansion, encircled by beds of deep pink Pride of Mobile azaleas, features original tiger oak floors, fireplaces, burled wood, and pocket French doors. The seasonal rose and azalea festivals unique to the Tyler area inspired the theme for The Seasons B&B. A talented artist, Myra painted wall murals and decorated the four guest rooms in keeping with the four seasons. The Spring Room creates the mood of an outdoor garden with its picket fence bed and murals of cascading flowers. The Winter Room features a Currier & Ives ice skating scene, a queen-size sleigh bed, and plush sheepskin rugs. Myra serves a gourmet breakfast. Sitting areas on the porches and in the garden encourage relaxation and serenity.

Historical Significance:

Samuel W. Littlejohn and his wife Anna built this lovely home in 1911. Mr. Littlejohn was the manager of Chronister Lumber Company, and the rare curly pine used in the woodwork throughout the first floor was milled especially for this house from local timber.

Places To Go, Sites To See:

Visit the nearby rose garden, antique shops, museums, theaters, Carnegie History Center, and the Caldwell Zoo. For a special treat, visit in March during the Azalea Trails Festival.

The Woldert-Spence Manor

611 West Woldert Street
Tyler, TX 75702-7149

800-Woldert
903-533-9057
Fax: 903-531-0293
E-Mail:
woldert-spence@tyler.net
Website:
www.tyler.net/woldert_spence

Hosts: Richard and Patricia
Heaton

BEDS: 4 rooms, 2 suites, 6 private baths

BREAKFAST & OTHER MEALS: Full breakfast

$$ Open all year

This beautifully restored two-story Queen Anne home is located on a large corner lot in the historic Brick Street District of Tyler. Original hardwood floors and stained-glass windows complement the carefully selected antique furnishings throughout the home. The guest rooms are elegant but inviting; two include a fireplace, others offer private balconies or screened-in porches. A television, VCR, telephone, and fax machine are available. The parlor houses an extensive library. In the rear garden, guests may enjoy a covered spa under huge shade trees along with a hammock, gazebo-covered wishing well, and a koi pool and fountains. The Heatons serve a bountiful, family-style breakfast in the formal dining room on antique china with background classical music.

Historical Significance:

The Woldert-Spence Manor is a Tyler Historical Landmark with roots that go back to the 1850s, when German immigrant, John George Woldert, came to Tyler with his family. Around 1910, when his granddaughter, Alma Mary Woldert, married Robert Spence (later the mayor of Tyler), the house underwent major remodeling including the addition of the second floor.

Places To Go, Sites To See:

The Manor is within walking distance of antique shops and minutes from Tyler Rose Garden, museums, lakes, and Caldwell Zoo.

Texas Stagecoach Inn

Hwy. 187
HC O2 Box 166
Vanderpool, TX 78885

888-965-6272
830-966-6272
E-Mail: stageinn@swtexas.net

Hosts: David and Karen Camp

BEDS: 3 rooms, 1 four-room suite, 4 private baths

BREAKFAST & OTHER MEALS: Full breakfast

$$, $$$ Open all year, two night minimum on weekends, three night minimum on holidays

At Texas Stagecoach Inn, David and Karen have created an idyllic hill country retreat. The two-story, 6000-square-foot home sits on three peaceful acres overlooking the Sabinal River. Decorated with "hill country elegance," the Inn offers a selection of guest rooms, from the upstairs Balcony Suite to the spacious ground floor rooms. The upstairs rooms open onto a large balcony that provides a spectacular view of the Hill Country. The Hitching Post Gift and Gallery features artwork by David and other area artists, as well as specialty gifts. The centerpiece of the Gallery is a massive fireplace constructed of rock from the river below. The enormous enclosed sun room overlooking the river provides a great place to read, relax, and enjoy this peaceful country setting.

Historical Significance:

In 1852, Bob Thompson was four years old when his family settled in The Sabinal Canyon. Bob built the original structure on this land in 1885. It burned in the 1890s, and in 1918 the home was rebuilt on the original foundation, then later expanded and remodeled to resemble an early Texas Stagecoach Inn. Today, five rooms of the original home, where Bob's eighteen children were reared, remain.

Places To Go, Sites To See:

Nature tourism is popular in this "undiscovered" area of the Texas Hill Country in all seasons. Vanderpool is the gateway to Lost Maples State Natural Area and Garner State Park. Enjoy abundant clear rivers, birding, wildlife, hiking, and scenic drives. Nearby are Bandera, the "Cowboy Capital of the World," and Medina, the "Apple Capital of Texas."

BonnyNook Inn

414 W. Main
Waxahachie, TX 75165

972-938-7207

Hosts: Bonnie and Vaughn
Franks

BEDS: 5 rooms, 5 private baths

BREAKFAST & OTHER MEALS: Full breakfast

$$ Open all year

The BonnyNook successfully combines Old World elegance with 20th-century amenities and couples classical Victorian authenticity in architecture and furnishings with modern creature comforts such as whirlpool tubs for two. The result is an eclectic collection of decorations and furnishings. Guests will discover comfortable beds, chairs and tables in each bedroom and a fully-stocked coffee nook in the hall. The exterior features the sunbursts, fish scales, bulls eyes, brackets and fretwork so popular with artisans of the Victorian period. BonnyNook's "Painted Lady" color scheme catches the eye, as do the garden plants of all shapes, sizes, colors, and textures.

Historical Significance:

When this 1887 Queen Anne Victorian was built, cotton and railroads were king. In 1890, Dr. W. West acquired the house and moved in with his wife, baby son, and his wife's sister. In 1896, Mrs. West was killed in a freak accident, and within three months Dr. West married his late wife's sister. Legend has it that ever since, the presence of the first Mrs. West has resided in one of the bedrooms.

Places To Go, Sites To See:

Ellis County Courthouse is the most photographed historic building in Texas, after the Alamo. The spring Gingerbread Trail and the Christmas tour of homes offer visitors a peek into the past. Scarborough Faire Renaissance Festival runs from late April until mid-June.

The Chaska House

716 West Main Street
Waxahachie, TX 75165

800-931-3390
972-937-3390

Hosts: Linda and Louis
Brown

BEDS: 2 rooms, 2 private baths, 3 room guest house with 3 private baths

BREAKFAST & OTHER MEALS: Full breakfast

$$, $$$ Open all year, two night minimum on holidays and special events weekends

With classic style, old-fashioned wrap-around verandas, and tree-shaded grounds, The Chaska House celebrates the joyous Revival style and attitude that flourished in turn-of-the-century Waxahachie when cotton was king. The house has been featured in *Texas Highways* and pictured in *House Beautiful* magazines. Guests enjoy romantic, spacious bedrooms with private baths, common rooms (parlor, library, grand hall) furnished with an extensive collection of American and European antiques, and elegant breakfasts served in the formal dining room. Louis and Linda often enliven breakfast conversation with local legends and inside tips.

Historical Significance:

Listed in the National Register of Historic Places, The Chaska House was built in 1900 by Edward and Marie Chaska, prosperous owners of the dry goods store they advertised as the "Emporium of Fashion" on the bustling town square. Boasting one of the largest concentrations of Gingerbread Victorian architecture in Texas, Waxahachie is a "sidewalk museum."

Places To Go, Sites To See:

The Chaska House is in the heart of Waxahachie's West End Historic District, an easy stroll to shopping, restaurants, the town square, and the famous courthouse James Michener called "A fairy tale palace...one of the finest buildings in Texas."

The Harrison Bed & Breakfast

717 W. Main
Waxahachie, TX 75165

972-938-1922
E-mail: slarkinbb@aol.com

Hosts: Sandee and Mark
Larkin

BEDS: 1 room, 1 suite, 1 cottage, 3 private baths

BREAKFAST & OTHER MEALS: Full or Continental Plus breakfast

$$$ Open all year

English country romance is the theme at this elegant Bed and Breakfast. Three spacious guest accommodations are tastefully appointed with European antiques, lush fabrics, family heirlooms, and "Harrison History." One suite has a private entrance from the veranda and a fireplace in the study. The Rendezvous Cottage is private and appealing, especially popular with honeymooners. Mark crafted an English potting shed with stained-glass windows and fine redwood paneling to enclose the new hot tub — private, romantic, inviting. Guests may enjoy the view from the veranda, curl up in a cozy chair in the study, or mingle with others in the living room or sunroom. Sandee serves a freshly prepared breakfast at midmorning. Sandee and Mark say, "Creating and rekindling marvelous memories for our guests is our goal. Come. . . enjoy!"

Historical Significance:

In 1915, James Wright Harrison built this stately home in the Mission Bungalow architectural style for his bride. Listed in the National Register of Historic Places, The Harrison stands proudly as one of the finest homes on Main Street.

Places To Go, Sites To See:

Enjoy Sandee's Coffee Chaser cookies and Harrison Hospitali-"tea," then stroll down to the courthouse square where you'll find antiquing and browsing at its best. Sandee claims Waxahachie has the most fun shops and friendly people in Texas.

The Rosemary Mansion On Main Street

903 W. Main Street
Waxahachie, TX 75165

972-935-9439
972-923-1181

Fax: 972-923-1199

Hosts: Judy and Dennis Cross

BEDS: 2 rooms, 2 suites, 4 private baths

BREAKFAST & OTHER MEALS: Full breakfast

$$, $$$ Open all year, two night minimum on holiday or special event weekends

Rosemary symbolizes remembrance and friendship. A visit to The Rosemary Mansion will indeed be a memorable experience for discerning guests. Diligently restored and lavishly decorated by Judy and Dennis, its fine art and period antique collections create a luxurious and tranquil setting. In the European tradition "with a Texas accent," guests are pampered with an evening welcoming party, tours of the manicured herb and rose gardens, and a bountiful herb-enhanced breakfast served on vintage china, crystal, and silver. Individually decorated guest rooms provide uncompromising comfort with old world charm. The Country Scented-Geranium Suite features a huge sitting room (the original sleeping porch) overlooking the back gardens. The French Lavender Bridal Suite is enormous and exquisitely furnished — perfect for a honeymoon or special occasion.

Historical Significance:

Listed in the National Register of Historic Places, this gracious Georgian Revival was built in 1916 for P.A. Chapman, a rancher, oilman, and banker. The family home was designed by architect C.W. Bulger, known for the first steel-framed Dallas skyscraper. One of the stunning, stately homes on Waxahachie's Main Street, it has been featured three times on the Gingerbread Trail tour of historic homes.

Places To Go, Sites To See:

Only twenty-seven miles from downtown Dallas, Waxahachie is an exciting city, boasting over twenty percent of all Nationally Registered Texas properties. Shopping, dining, sightseeing, and recreational opportunities abound in the area.

Thee Hubbell House

307 West Elm Street
Winnsboro, TX 75494

800-227-0639
903-342-5629
Fax: 903-342-6627
E-Mail:
hubhouse@bluebonnet.net
Website:
www.bluebonnet.net/hubhouse

Hosts: Dan and Laurel Hubbell

BEDS: 12 rooms, 12 private baths

BREAKFAST & OTHER MEALS: Full or Continental breakfast; candlelight dinners by reservation only

$, $$, $$$ Open all year

Located in Winnsboro's historic district, Thee Hubbell House is a Recorded Texas Historic Landmark. Guest accommodations are in three historic houses on a two-acre landscaped plantation estate. Luxuriously appointed common areas in the Mansion include a formal living room with a piano and fireplace, dining room, and entry hall. The Carriage House caters to business travelers or those who desire more privacy, and continental breakfasts and coffee makers are provided in these rooms. Spacious verandas and garden sitting areas nestled among the southern magnolia, oak, and pecan trees encourage relaxation. A private "Hot Tub House" is available by reservation.

Historical Significance:

The original part of the plantation Mansion was constructed in 1888. Confederate Colonel J.A. Stinson purchased the property in 1906 and determined its present Colonial style. Colonel Stinson's oldest daughter married Governor James Hogg, and they became the parents of the famous philanthropist, Ima Hogg, who frequently visited the estate.

Places To Go, Sites To See:

Thee Hubbell House is within walking distance of the downtown shops and antique malls. Explore the scenic East Texas lake country with over 100 antique shops, 7 golf courses, 10 lakes, and excellent restaurants within a 30 minute drive.

Famous and Favorite
Innkeepers' Recipes

Blintz Soufflé with Blueberry Topping
(Ant Street Inn/Brenham)

1 cup flour
1/3 cup sugar
2 tsp. baking powder
1/2 tsp. cinnamon
1-1/2 cups sour cream
1/2 cup orange juice

1 8-oz. package cream cheese, softened
16 oz. small curd cottage cheese
7 eggs
1/4 cup butter, softened
1 tsp. vanilla

Mix dry ingredients in large mixing bowl. Add remaining ingredients and beat until thoroughly mixed.

Pour into a 9" x 13" greased baking dish or two smaller casserole dishes. Cover and refrigerate overnight, or for at least 2 hours. Bake in a pre-heated oven at 350° for 50-65 minutes. Serve.

Blueberry Sauce

1 cup sugar
Dash of salt
1/4 tsp. nutmeg
5 tbsp. cornstarch

1 cup boiling water
1 cup blueberries, fresh or thawed frozen
1 tbsp. lemon juice

Mix dry ingredients in saucepan. Add 1 cup boiling water and stir. Heat to a boil, stirring constantly. Add blueberries and stir until thickened. Remove from heat and add lemon juice. Serve on top of soufflé.

Serves: 20

Hot Spiced Fruit
(The Oxford House/Stephenville)

1 29-oz. can of pears
1 29-oz. can of apricot halves
1 29-oz. can of freestone peaches
1/2 cup chopped nuts, optional
1/2 cup raisins, optional

1/2 cup frozen orange juice
2 tbsp. melted butter
1/2 cup brown sugar
1/2 tsp. cinnamon
Nutmeg and cloves to taste

Drain fruits well; add nuts and raisins. Arrange in a greased baking dish. Pour orange juice and melted butter on top. Sprinkle with brown sugar and spices. Bake at 350° for 30 minutes.

Serves: 8-10

Grapefruit á la Texas
(Bailey House/Bay City)

2 grapefruit
4 tbsp. brown sugar
Maraschino cherries

Turn on broiler. Slice grapefruit in half, then section and remove center from fruit. Sprinkle 1 tbsp. brown sugar over top of each grapefruit half. Arrange on broiler pan and place under broiler until sugar melts and edges of grapefruit turn delicate brown. Remove from broiler and place cherry in center of each half. Serve at once.

Serves: 4

Cookies 'n' Cream Cheesecake
(Ant Street Inn/Brenham)

2-2/3 cups crumbled chocolate sandwich cookies (28)
1/3 cup butter, melted
3 8-oz. packages cream cheese
1 14-oz. can sweetened condensed milk

3 eggs	1-1/2 cups sour cream
1 tbsp. vanilla	2 tbsp. sugar
16 chocolate cookies, coarsely crumbled	1/2 tsp. vanilla

Combine cookie crumbs and butter, press firmly on bottom and halfway up sides of a 9" springform pan. Chill.

Beat cream cheese until fluffy in a large mixing bowl, gradually beat in condensed milk until smooth. Stir in eggs, mixing well. Add 1 tbsp. vanilla. Fold in crumbled cookies. Pour mixture into cheesecake pan. Bake at 400° for 5 minutes, reduce temperature to 325° and continue baking for 55-60 minutes longer.

Mix sour cream, sugar, and 1/2 tsp. vanilla. Gently spoon over cheesecake and spread evenly. Bake an additional 10 minutes. Cool to room temperature. Cover and chill overnight.

Editors Note: This recipe is an award winning recipe recognized by French chef Jacques Fox (Executive Chef, University of Houston Culinary Department) and served by his staff at the 1996 HAT Annual Conference.

Serves: 12

Plum Cake with Bourbon Glaze
(Countryside Inn/Martindale)

2 cups self-rising flour	3 eggs
2 cups sugar	1 tsp. cinnamon
2 jars baby food, plums	1 tsp. cloves
1 cup canola oil	1 cup chopped nuts

Combine all ingredients in large bowl. Mix at medium speed until well blended — do not overbeat. Bake in greased and floured bundt pan at 350° for about 1 hour. While cake is still hot, top with glaze.

Glaze
1/3 cup bourbon
1/3 cup powdered sugar

Mix well.

Cook's Note: Cake freezes well for use during busy times!

Yield: one 12" cake

Southwestern Eggs with Broiled Tomatoes
(Crystal River Inn/San Marcos)

10 eggs	1/2 cup flour
1 tsp. baking powder	1 tsp. salt
1/2 pound grated Monterey Jack	1-1/2 cups cottage cheese
8 oz. chopped green canned chilis	1 stick melted butter

Beat eggs well, then whisk in salt, baking powder, and flour. Fold in cheeses and chilis. Finally, stir in melted butter and bake in greased and floured 9" x 13" casserole at 350° for 35-40 minutes. It will just be turning brown — don't overbake. Top with your favorite salsa, a few crumbles of goat cheese, and a sprig of cilantro.

Broiled tomatoes (good for luncheon and dinner side dish, also): Slice five tomatoes in half and paint with melted butter. Dust with garlic powder, a sprinkle of basil, and a lot of parmesan cheese. Broil for 8-10 minutes under moderate heat, until bubbly, brown, and soft.

Serves: 8-10

Baked Pears
(Das Garten Haus/Fredericksburg)

4 ripe Bartlett pears	I tsp. cinnamon
3/4 cup oats	6 tbsp. butter
3/4 cup brown sugar	2 small (6-oz.) cans of apple juice
1/2 tsp. nutmeg	

Core pears but do not peel. Place in greased 9" square pan. Combine oats, sugar, spices, and butter until crumbly. Stuff pears letting excess fall into pan. Pour in one can apple juice. Bake at 350° for one hour, basting after 30 minutes. You may need to add more juice at this point. Cool 30 minutes before serving with a little cream.

Serves: 4

Bread Pudding with Cream Cheese & Cinnamon
(Karbach Haus Bed & Breakfast Home/New Braunfels)

On the day before you plan to serve it, cream together the following ingredients:

1 8-oz. package cream cheese	1/2 tsp. vanilla
1 cup sugar	1 tsp. cinnamon

Spread this mixture on 6 slices of day old soft-crusted sourdough or French bread. Cover with 6 more slices of bread, making sandwiches. Slice or tear the sandwiches into bite-size squares and pile them into a 9" x 13" buttered casserole dish, or one that has been sprayed with Pam.

In a large mixing bowl, blend together:

12 eggs	1/2 cup sugar
2 cups milk	1/2 tsp. salt
4 oz. cream cheese	1/4 cup butter (melted and cooled)

Beat eggs until light and fluffy. Add remaining ingredients and blend well. Pour over bread and cream cheese mixture in baking dish. Cover with foil or plastic wrap and refrigerate overnight.

Next morning: Cover with 1/2 cup chopped pecans and bake at 375° for 45 minutes. Serve with powdered sugar or your favorite topping.

Serves: 12

Special Scrambled Eggs
(Countryside Inn/Martindale)

3 tbsp. butter or oleo
1/2 cup milk
12 eggs
2 tsp. chopped fresh chives

1/4 tsp. salt
3-oz. cream cheese, cut in small cubes
2-oz. jar pimentos, drained, *or*
   1 large tomato, peeled and chopped

In skillet, melt butter. In bowl, beat milk and eggs until light. Stir in chives, salt and pepper. Pour egg mixture into melted butter and cook over medium heat until eggs begin to set. Add cream cheese — continue cooking, stirring occasionally, until cream cheese is melted and eggs are set. Fold in pimentos and serve.

Serves: 6-8

Sausage Biscuits
(The Oxford House/Stephenville)

3/4 lb. hot/mild bulk pork sausage
2-2/3 cups all-purpose flour
2 tbsp. sugar
1 tsp. baking powder
1/2 tsp. baking soda
1/2 tsp. salt

1/2 cup shortening
1 package dry yeast
1/4 cup warm water (105 - 115°)
1 cup buttermilk
1/2 cup melted butter or margarine

Cook sausage in a skillet until browned, stirring to crumble. Drain well and set aside.

Combine the flour, sugar, baking powder, baking soda, and salt, mixing well. Cut in shortening with a pastry blender until mixture resembles course meal. Dissolve yeast in warm water; let stand for 5 minutes. Add yeast mixture to buttermilk, stirring well; add to dry ingredients. Stir just until moistened. Knead in sausage. Turn dough out onto a lightly floured surface; knead lightly for about 4 minutes.

Roll dough to 1/2" thickness; cut with a 1-3/4" round cutter. Place biscuits on an ungreased baking sheet. Brush tops with melted butter. Bake in pre-heated 425° oven for 10 minutes or until golden brown.

Cook's Note: To freeze, place uncooked biscuits on an ungreased baking sheet; cover and freeze until firm. Transfer frozen biscuits to plastic bags. To bake, place frozen biscuits on ungreased baking sheet and bake as above.

Yield: 3 dozen biscuits

Pecan Crusted Bacon
(The Luckenbach Inn/Fredericksburg)

Bacon strips
Maple syrup
Pecans

Heat oven to 400°. Place bacon strips on cookie sheet lined with parchment paper.Brush top side of bacon with maple syrup. Sprinkle with finely chopped pecans. Bake until desired crispness.

Yield: depends on how many bacon strips used

The Governors' Inn Granola
(The Governors' Inn/Austin)

6 cups oatmeal
1 cup wheat germ
1 cup All-Bran cereal
1 cup nuts
1 cup coconut
1/2 cup brown sugar
1 tsp. cinnamon
1 cup honey
1/2 cup oil

Mix together first five ingredients. Add brown sugar and cinnamon and mix well. In a separate bowl, combine honey and oil and heat slightly to blend (~45 seconds in microwave). Stir honey and oil and pour over the dry ingredients. MIX WELL. Bake at 300° for 25-30 minutes, STIRRING EVERY 10 MINUTES.

Serves: 24

Yvonne's French Toast
(Das College Haus/Fredericksburg)

4 slices multi-grain or honey wheat bread
4 oz. cream cheese, cubed into bite size pieces
4 eggs
1 cup milk
1/2 cup maple syrup
1 tsp. vanilla
2 tsp. cinnamon

Cube the 4 slices of multi-grain or honey wheat bread. Spray bottom of square casserole with Pam and put cubed bread into pan. Top with cubed cream cheese. Mix eggs, milk, maple syrup, vanilla, and cinnamon in separate bowl. Pour mixture over top of bread cubes. Refrigerate for several hours, or overnight. Bake at 350° for about 50 minutes. Serve with additional maple syrup.

Serves: 4

Crispy Potato Quiche
(McLachlan Farm Bed & Breakfast/Spring)

1 24-oz. package frozen shredded hashbrowns (thawed)	
1/3 cup melted butter/margarine	1/2 cup Half & Half
1 cup shredded jalapeno cheese	2 eggs
1 cup shredded Swiss cheese	1/4 tsp. salt
4-5 oz. diced cooked ham	Cayenne Pepper (to taste)
1/2-1 bunch green onions, chopped	

Press thawed hashbrowns between paper towels to remove moisture. Press potatoes into greased 10" pie plate and brush with melted butter. Bake at 425° for 25 minutes. Remove from oven. In the baked potato crust, layer cheeses, ham and onions.

Beat Half & Half with eggs, salt and pepper, and pour over the cheese. Bake uncovered 40-50 minutes in 350° oven or until knife comes out clean.

Serves: 6

Walnut Salad Dressing
(Moonlight Bay B&B/Palacios)

2 green onions	1 tsp. salt
6 sprigs fresh parsley	Scant 1/2 tsp. white pepper
1/4 cup finely chopped walnuts	2 tsp. paprika
1-1/2 cups plus 2 tbsp. mayonnaise	Scant 1/2 tsp. dried tarragon leaves
6 tbsp. buttermilk	4 tsp. sugar
1-1/2 tsp. minced fresh garlic	1-1/2 tbsp. tarragon vinegar

Wash green onions and parsley and shake dry, then pat dry with paper towels. Chop 1/2 inch off the ends of green onions and discard. Whittle leaves off parsley. Chop onions and parsley leaves finely by hand, then combine with remaining ingredients and mix well. Refrigerate in a tightly covered container.

Serve this smooth, mellow dressing over mixed greens garnished with fresh tomatoes, alfalfa sprouts and croutons.

Editors Note: This recipe is an award winning recipe recognized by French chef Jacques Fox (Executive Chef, University of Houston Culinary Department) and served by his staff at the 1996 HAT Annual Conference.

Yield: 2 cups

Grandma's Gingerbread Men
(Schildknecht-Weidenfeller House/Fredericksburg)

Thoroughly mix the following seven dry ingredients:

5 to 5-1/2 cups all-purpose flour

1 tsp. baking soda	2 tsp. cinnamon
1 tsp. salt	1 tsp. nutmeg
2 tsp. ginger	1 tsp. cloves

Melt in large saucepan:

1 cup shortening

Add to melted shortening and mix well:

1 cup sugar

2 eggs, beaten

1-1/4 cups unsulphured molasses

Cool slightly, then add 4 cups of the dry ingredients and mix well. Turn mixture onto lightly floured surface. Knead remaining dry ingredients by hand. Roll dough to 1/8" thickness. Cut out pieces with a gingerbread cutter or knife. Place on greased cookie sheets. Bake at 375° for 8-10 minutes. Cool on cookie sheets a few minutes. Remove and cool completely on rack. Decorate as desired.

Cook's Note: Our family loves these little gingerbread men made from Grandma's recipe. We'd like to share this taste from the past with you. When you visit the Schildknecht-Weidenfeller House, you will find a plate of these waiting for you!

Yield: number of cookies depends on size of gingerbread men that are cut out.

The Orchard Inn's Brunch Fruit
(The Orchard Inn/Fredericksburg)

1 can cherry pie filling	1 12-oz. package prunes (pitted)
2-1/2 cups water	1 11-oz. package apricots (dried)
1/4 cup sugar	1 13.5-oz. pineapple chunks (undrained)

Mix cherry pie filling, water, and sugar. Add fruits. Cook covered on high in microwave for 10 minutes. Then cook on medium high for 20 minutes, stirring after 10 minutes. Delicious hot or cold.

Cook's Note: This is a great warm winter fruit dish! We top the individual servings with a spoonful of black cherry yogurt.

Serves: 10-12

Best Tenderloin (Always Perfect!)
(Moonlight Bay B&B/Palacios)

2 tsp. salt
2 tsp. garlic powder
1 tsp. black pepper

1/4 cup Major Grey's Mango Chutney (heated)
One strip pork tenderloin or beef tenderloin

PORK:

Preheat oven to 500°. Combine salt, garlic powder, and black pepper in plastic bag. Add one strip of pork tenderloin and shake well until completely coated.

Spray metal pan with Pam, then add meat. Cook in hot oven for 10 minutes. Turn oven off. DO NOT OPEN FOR 4 HOURS.

Use electric knife to slant cut meat. Arrange 3 slices per person and pour heated chutney over meat.

BEEF:

Repeat all steps above except when putting meat in oven, turn heat off immediately. Use packaged Bernaise sauce over meat.

Serves: 6-8

Settlement Breakfast Cookies
(The Settlement at Round Top)

1 cup brown sugar
1 cup white sugar
1 cup shortening
2 eggs, beaten
1 tsp. vanilla
2 cups (scant) flour
1 tsp. salt

1 tsp. baking powder
1 tsp. baking soda in 1 tbsp. hot water
2 cups quick rolled oats (oatmeal)
1 cup Wheaties
1 cup chopped nuts
1/4 cup wheat germ

Mix all together and bake at 350° for 10 minutes, or until done. When cool, frost with the following:

1 cup oleo
1 tsp. maple extract
4 cups powdered sugar
Milk as needed to make a spreading consistency

Yield: 24 cookies

Spinach Quiche
(The McCallum House/Austin)

Blend well:

1 cup low fat condensed milk (evaporated skim)
4 eggs
2 tbsp. chopped green onion
1 tbsp. flour
1/4 tsp. nutmeg
1-1/2 tsp. dried chives or dried onion
1/4 tsp. each seasoned salt & white pepper

Distribute evenly in "PAMed" pie plate:

1 cup shredded Swiss cheese
4 slices cooked crumbled bacon
1 10-oz. package frozen spinach, thawed and drained

Top with egg mixture. Bake at 350° for 30 minutes. (Also good without bacon or with bacon bits crumbled on top.)

Serves: 6-8

Artichoke and Olive Squares
(Noble Inns/San Antonio)

1 tbsp. minced onion flakes *or* 1/4 cup finely chopped onion
1/2 cup water
4 eggs, beaten
1/4 cup seasoned breadcrumbs
1/4 tsp. oregano
2-3 drops hot pepper sauce
1 lb. Cheddar or Colby-Jack cheese, shredded
12 oz. marinated artichoke hearts, drained and chopped
4 oz. sliced black olives, drained

Cook onion in water until tender (about 5 minutes), then drain. In a large bowl, beat eggs; blend in breadcrumbs, oregano and hot pepper sauce. Stir in onion, cheese, artichoke hearts and olives. Spread in a greased 7-1/2" x 11" pan. Bake at 350° for 18 minutes. Let cool slightly to set, then cut into 1" squares and serve warm.

Serves: 12-15

Almond Praline Pumpkin Pie
(Pearl Street Inn Bed & Breakfast/Granbury)

1 14-oz. can sweetened condensed milk
1 15-oz. can Pumpkin
2 tsp. pumpkin pie spice
1 deep dish pie crust or quiche pan pie crust

2 eggs
1/4 tsp. almond extract
1/4 tsp. vanilla extract
Almond Topping

Combine sweetened condensed milk, pumpkin, eggs, pumpkin pie spice, and flavorings; stir until well blended. Pour pumpkin mixture into pie crust. Bake at 425° for 15 minutes. Reduce oven temperature to 350° and bake an additional 30 minutes. Regular pie shell crust may need to have edges covered with strips of aluminum foil to prevent excessive browning; quiche pan should not. Remove from oven and carefully spoon Almond Topping evenly over top of pie. Return to oven and bake an additional 10-15 minutes or until golden brown. Let cool. Serve warm or chilled.

Almond Topping
2 tbsp. firmly packed dark brown sugar
1 egg lightly beaten
2 tbsp. light corn syrup
1 tbsp. butter, melted
1 cup slivered almonds, toasted

Combine first 4 ingredients, stirring well. Stir in almonds.

Cook's Note: This recipe is the 1997 Harvest Moon Blue Ribbon Pie Recipe!

Yield: one 9" pie.

Southwestern Quiche
(The McCallum House/Austin)

Reduce by half and then cool: 1 10-oz. can diced tomatoes & green chilis (Rotel).

Combine thoroughly:

4 eggs, beaten
1 cup milk, skim
3 tbsp. Parmesan cheese
2 cups shredded Swiss or Monterey Jack cheese

Salt and pepper to taste
1 tbsp. dried basil
1/2 tsp. garlic powder

Add cooled tomato mixture to egg mixture. Combine well. Pour into "PAMed" glass pie plate. Bake at 350° for about 30 minutes.

Serves: 6-8

Asparagus Tea Sandwiches
(The Oxford House/Stephenville)

1 can (small) asparagus
1 8-oz. package cream cheese (softened)
1 boiled egg
1 loaf white bread
1/2 cup melted butter
1/2 cup parmesan cheese

Mix asparagus, cream cheese, and boiled egg. Cut crust off of bread slices and spread mixture, making sandwiches. Cut sandwiches into quarters. Roll each quarter in butter, then in parmesan cheese. (Can be frozen at this point on an ungreased cookie sheet.) Bake at 400° for 8 to 10 minutes or until brown.

Yield: 20-30 sandwiches

Vegetarian Frittata
(Rosevine Inn Bed & Breakfast/Tyler)

3 new potatoes
2 tsp. cooking oil
1 yellow squash
1 zucchini squash
3 mushrooms
1 small yellow onion
1 tomato
2 tsp. olive oil or butter

4 eggs
1 tbsp. parmesan cheese (grated)
1/3 cup milk
1/8 tsp. oregano
Salt & pepper to taste
Any cheese (optional)

Clean and cube potatoes. Cook in a 10" iron skillet until done. Drain and set aside. Spray pan with a non-stick spray. Cube squash and tomato. Slice mushrooms and chop the onion. Saute all the vegetables, except tomato, in the olive oil or butter until tender. Beat eggs and milk until frothy; add parmesan cheese, oregano, salt & pepper — mix well. Add potatoes and tomato to the other vegetables in the skillet and stir together. Pour egg mixture over the vegetables. Cook over medium heat, lifting edges as the eggs cook. When eggs are set, sprinkle optional cheese over the top and put under broiler until it just starts to brown. Garnish as desired. Cut into pie-shaped wedges and serve from the pan.

Cook's Note: If meat is desired, smoked sausage is an excellent choice!!

Serves: 4-6

Pumpkin Pancakes With Praline Syrup
(Texas Stagecoach Inn/Vanderpool)

1 cup flour
2 tbsp. sugar
Dash of salt
2 tsp. baking powder
1 cup milk
2 tsp. vegetable oil
1 egg
1 tsp. cinnamon
1 cup canned pumpkin
1/2 cup sour cream
1 8-oz. package cream cheese (softened)

In a large bowl, combine all ingredients except cream cheese. Bake pancakes on a heated griddle until edges are brown and bubbles rise to the surface; then turn and bake until golden. The pancakes are very light. After cooking, spread each pancake with cream cheese and roll like a crepe. Serve with hot Praline Sauce.

Praline Sauce: Combine 1 cup toasted walnuts (chopped), 2 sticks butter, and 2/3 cup honey in a saucepan. Heat to boiling (thick boiling). Serve warm over pancakes.

Serves: 4-6

Lemon Ice Cream and Fresh Fruit
(Heart Of My Heart Ranch/Round Top)

1-1/2 gallon container
3 qts. Half & Half
1 cup whipping cream
Juice 12 lemons
Grate lemon rinds
3 tsp. lemon extract
3 cups sugar

Mix ingredients together, then freeze (in freezer overnight). Serve in chilled wine glass with fresh fruit of choice.

Yield: 16-20 glasses

Brunch Eggs & Green Chilies
(Historic Kuebler-Waldrip Haus & Danville School/New Braunfels)

2 4-oz. cans chopped green chilies
1 lb. chopped Cheddar cheese
6 - 7 whole eggs

1-1/2 cups Pioneer Biscuit Mix
1 qt. milk (whole or 2%)
3/4 tsp. salt

Lightly grease the desired size dish, then line a 9" x 13" dish, two round 8" dishes, or three 6" single dishes with chilies. Layer cheese on top. Beat eggs with Biscuit Mix, milk, and salt; pour over cheese and chilies.

Bake for 1 hour at 350° (less for glass dish) or until brown.

Cook's Note: Use of a microwave is not suggested for this dish — it will come out much better if cooked only in a conventional oven.

Serves: 10-12

German Pancakes
(Munzesheimer Manor/Mineola)

6 large eggs
1 cup all-purpose flour
1 cup milk
1/4 cup melted butter

1 tsp. salt
1/2 cup powdered sugar
6 lemon wedges
12 pre-cooked link sausage

Batter: Beat eggs in mixer on "high" for 5 minutes. Alternately add the flour and milk. Add melted butter. Add salt. Continue to mix ingredients for another minute.

Spray 6 oval au gratin baking dishes with Baker's Joy. Ladle 4 oz. of batter into each baking dish (a large kitchen ladle is about 4 oz.). Bake in oven at 425° between 10 - 15 minutes (make certain they don't burn).

Heat sausage links according to instructions on package (usually in 2 - 3 tbsp. water in a skillet over low heat for 5 - 10 minutes). Remove pancakes from oven when golden brown and sprinkle with powdered sugar. Place two sausages inside each pancake. Serve on a plate with one lemon wedge, a fruit garnish, and syrup.

Cook's Note: We usually use a "strawberry fan" as garnish and Norris' Moonshine Syrup.

Serves: 6

Peach Filling For Crepes
(Magnolia House/Fredericksburg)

1 8-oz. package cream cheese (softened)
1/2 cup sugar (sometimes we also add 1 or 2 tsp. cottage cheese)
1 tsp. vanilla
1/4 cup soft butter
1/4 cup brown sugar
6 large peaches (sliced)

Combine cream cheese, sugar and vanilla. Beat until smooth. Spread cream cheese mixture over crepe. Place a row of sliced peaches on each crepe. Dot with butter and sugar. Roll up crepes and place in 13" x 9" x 2" pan. Bake at 325° for 8 to 10 minutes.

Yield: enough for 8-10 crepes

Stuffed French Toast With Apricot Glaze
(The Pelican House/Seabrook)

1 8-oz. package cream cheese (softened)
1 8-oz. can crushed pineapple
1/4 cup pecans
6 eggs
1 tsp. vanilla
1 cup milk
1 tsp. ginger
Small jar of apricot preserves
1/2 cup orange juice
1 loaf French bread

Stuffing: Combine cream cheese, crushed pineapple and pecans.

Batter: Beat eggs; then add vanilla, milk and ginger.

Apricot Glaze: Combine apricot preserves and orange juice in saucepan, then bring to boil.

Cut French bread into 2-inch slices. Cut pockets into center of each bread slice and add a heaping tablespoon of stuffing. Batter stuffed slices and fry in butter. Top with Apricot Glaze.

Yield: 8-10 slices

Christmas Eggs
(Bolin's Prairie House/Abilene)

1 lb. sausage — cooked and drained	12 eggs
4 oz. can sliced mushrooms	1 cup milk
1/2 cup green onions — chopped	1-1/2 tsp. salt
2 medium tomatoes — chopped	1/2 tsp. pepper
2 cups (8 oz.) shredded Mozzarella cheese	1/2 tsp. dried oregano
1-1/4 cups Bisquick	

Grease a 9" x 13" pan. Layer sausage, mushrooms, green onion, tomatoes, and cheese. (You may cover and refrigerate overnight at this point, or continue and bake immediately).

Beat remaining ingredients and pour over layers.

Bake uncovered in 350° oven until golden brown and set — about 30 minutes.

Serves: 8-10

Belgian New Year's Cakes
(The Delforge Place/Fredericksburg)

1 lb. butter
1 lb. eggs (8 large or 10 small)
1 lb. flour (4 cups)
1 lb. sugar (2 cups white sugar and 1-1/8 cups brown sugar)

Batter: Cream butter and sugar; add flour and egg yolks. Beat egg whites until frothy. Fold into mixture and refrigerate overnight.

Spoon tablespoon of batter (it will be sticky, so flour your hands) onto heated heart-shaped waffle iron (makes 5 at a time) or other decorative-shaped waffle iron. Bake for 1 to 2 minutes, maximum. Remove and let cool on wax paper. (Will keep in refrigerator for up to 3 or 4 weeks).

Cook's Note: This recipe was handed down from the Delforge's Belgian ancestry. The New Year's Cakes are served as a pastry in the morning with jam and coffee, sprinkled with confectioners' sugar and served with iced tea in the afternoon, and served plain in the evening with wine. Legend says they bring good luck for the coming year!

Yield: 7 dozen

Pumpkin Pancakes
(Pearl Street Inn Bed & Breakfast/Granbury)

2 cups biscuit mix	1-1/2 cup evaporated milk
2 tbsp. packed brown sugar	1/2 cup solid pack pumpkin
2 tsp. ground cinnamon	2 tbsp. vegetable oil
1/4 tsp. nutmeg	2 eggs
1 tsp. ground allspice	1 tsp. vanilla extract

Combine biscuit mix, sugar, cinnamon, nutmeg and allspice in large mixing bowl. Add evaporated milk, pumpkin, oil, eggs, and vanilla; beat until smooth. Pour 1/4 to 1/2 cupfuls onto lightly greased heated griddle. Cook until top surface is bubbly and edges are dry, then turn. Serve with honey or syrup of choice.

Serves: approximately 8 persons

Bananas Foster Crepes
(Crystal River Inn/San Marcos)

1/2 stick butter, melted (1/4 cup)	1 cup sour cream
1 cup brown sugar (packed)	2 tsp. whipping cream
1 tsp. pumpkin pie spice	1 packet artificial sweetner
4 tbsp. Grand Marnier or Triple Sec	Toasted almonds
3 bananas	Mint sprigs

Make a batch of 12 large, pretty crepes. This can be done ahead of time. When ready to use, warm them.

Filling: Melt 1/2 stick of butter. Stir in brown sugar. Add enough water to make a thin syrup. Allow to simmer briskly until partly reduced. Add pumpkin pie spice and Grand Marnier or Triple Sec. Allow to simmer 1 to 2 minutes. Slice in 3 bananas. Simmer until they wilt – about 5 minutes.

Creme Topping: Stir together sour cream, whipping cream, and artificial sweetener.

Assembly: Fill each crepe with 4 to 6 banana slices and wrap it closed, placing seam down on the serving plate. Place a second crepe alongside. Top the twosome with liberal pan syrup, a dollop of creme topping, toasted almonds, banana slice, and sprig of mint. Serve with sausage, Mimosas, and gourmet coffee.

Serves: 6 people

Guadalupe Ranch Roasted Onion, Sweet Pepper & Corn Soup
(Guadalupe River Ranch/Boerne)

4 very large sweet onions
1 red, yellow and green peppers
1 ear sweet corn (stripped)
2 tsp. fresh thyme
1 tsp. fresh marjoram
4 bay leaves
1 tbsp. black peppercorn
2 tbsp. minced fresh garlic

2 tbsp. dark chili powder
1/4 cup white & red wines
1 qt. total beef and chicken broth
Salt & pepper to taste
4 slices Parmesan cheese
1/2 cup croutons
4 scallions (for garnish)

Hollow out onions to use as bowls. Slice peppers and set aside a few slices of each for garnish. Roast pepper seeds, remaining pepper slices, and corn kernels in oven (or saucepan on medium) until corn is brown and tender. Make a bouquet garni with thyme, marjoram, bay leaves and peppercorn by placing in a small piece of cheesecloth and tying with string. Saute garlic and remaining onion; add wines and stir while wine reduces by half. Add beef and chicken broth, roasted corn and peppers, chili powder and bouquet garni. Simmer 30 minutes.

Place onion bowls on kosher salt or uncooked rice to hold in place. Fill with hot soup. Cover with croutons, top with Parmesan cheese. Bake at 375° for 12-15 minutes or until cheese begins to brown. Garnish with fresh pepper strips and insert scallion flower.

Serves: 4

Orange Fluff
(Brackenridge House "a bed and breakfast inn"/San Antonio)

1 6-oz. can concentrated orange juice
1 cup milk (*we use skim or 2% milk*)
1 cup water
1 or 2 tsp. vanilla
1/4 cup sugar
Enough ice cubes to fill a standard-size blender

Whirl ingredients in blender and serve immediately!

Serves: 6-8

Orange Pecan French Toast
(The Woldert-Spence Manor/Tyler)

5 eggs
2/3 cup orange juice
1/3 cup milk
1/4 cup sugar
1/2 tsp. ground nutmeg
1/2 tsp. vanilla extract

1/4 cup Triple Sec Liquor (orange)
1/2 loaf (8 oz.) French bread, cut in 1" slices
1/3 cup (5-1/2 tbs.) butter — melted
1/2 cup pecan pieces (or walnuts)
Grated orange peel to taste, about 2 tbsp.

Using wire wisk, beat together eggs, orange juice, milk, sugar, nutmeg, vanilla, and Triple Sec. Place bread with edges touching in a single layer in a large flat dish. Pour milk mixture over bread, cover, and refrigerate overnight, turning once.

When ready to cook, pre-heat oven to 400° Fahrenheit. Spray jelly roll pan with vegetable spray. Pour melted butter on jelly roll pan, spreading evenly. Arrange soaked bread slices in a single layer on pan. Sprinkle evenly with orange peel and pecans.

Bake until golden, 20 - 25 minutes. Check slices during last 10 minutes of baking to avoid burning. Serve with maple syrup and butter, or fresh fruits.

Cook's Note: Use only soft crust French bread; spray only with Pam.

Serves: 4

Egg/Sausage Casserole
(Heather's Glen... A Bed & Breakfast and More!/Conroe)

1 lb. sausage roll (regular)
2 4-oz. cans drained green chilies (chopped)
4 cups shredded Cheddar cheese
2 cups milk (use regular, not skim milk)

1 cup Bisquick
6 eggs
9" x 13" pan

Brown sausage and drain, then put in dish. Sprinkle green chilies and cheese over sausage. Separately, beat milk and eggs together; then mix in Bisquick. Pour mixture over sausage/cheese. Bake at 350° for 30 minutes. Cut into squares to serve.

Cook's Note: Save time by cooking sausage ahead of time!

Serves: 8-10

The Captain's Baked Eggs
(Bed & Breakfast On The Bay/Kemah)

7 eggs	2/3 cup butter or margarine (melted)
1 cup milk	1/2 cup flour
2 tsp. sugar	1 tsp. baking powder
4 oz. cubed cream cheese	Dash of paprika
1 lb. small curd cottage cheese	Dash of ground mustard

1 lb. shredded Monterey Jack or Muenster cheese
1/4 cup chopped green peppers or pimiento (optional)

Beat together eggs, milk, and sugar. Add cheeses, chopped peppers, and melted butter; mix well. Mix in flour, baking powder, paprika, and ground mustard, then pour into 3-quart baking dish sprayed with non-stick pan coating. Bake 45 to 50 minutes at 350°, or until knife comes out clean from center. (May be prepared in advance, then covered and refrigerated – if put in oven directly from refrigerator, uncover and bake up to 60 minutes.) Cut into rectangles to serve.

Serves: 12

Apple Cheese Breakfast Clafouti
(Weinert House/Seguin)

1 can apple pie filling or topping
1 cup shredded Cheddar cheese
4 eggs
1-1/4 cup light cream
1/2 tsp. vanilla
2/3 cup all-purpose flour
2 tbsp. sugar
1/4 tsp. nutmeg, plus additional amount for garnish
1/8 tsp. salt (optional)

Heat oven to 350°. Spread pie filling in a 12" x 8" (2-qt.) baking dish; sprinkle with cheese. Beat together eggs, cream, and vanilla. In a separate bowl, stir together flour, sugar, netmeg, and salt. Add dry mixture to liquid mixture. Pour over apples and cheese. Sprinkle with additional nutmeg to garnish. Bake at 350° for 50 to 60 minutes, or until wooden toothpick inserted near center comes out clean. Clafouti will be very puffy and will collapse as it cools. Remove from oven and cool 15 minutes. Serve warm.

Serves: 4-6

Cranberry Apple Muffins
(Angel Arbor Bed & Breakfast Inn/Houston)

1-1/2 cups all-purpose flour
1 tsp. baking soda
1 tsp. cinnamon
1/4 tsp. salt
2 large eggs
1 cup packed brown sugar

1/4 cup oil
1 tsp. vanilla
1 cup diced, unpeeled apple
1 cup fresh cranberries
1/2 cup coarsely chopped walnuts

Heat oven to 350°. Grease a 12-cup muffin pan. Mix flour, baking soda, cinnamon and salt in a large bowl.

Beat eggs in another bowl. Add sugar and beat again. Whisk in oil and vanilla. Stir in apple, cranberries and walnuts. Pour over dry ingredients (previous bowl) and fold in just until moistened. Spoon batter into muffin cups and bake 20-25 minutes, or until one muffin center tests done.

Yield: 12 muffins

Stuffed French Toast
(Old Hunter Road Stagecoach Inn/New Braunfels)

1 8-oz. package cream cheese (softened)
3 tbsp. apricot marmalade
1 tbsp. sour cream
3/4 cup Mozzarella cheese
8 2-inch slices of Sourdough French Bread
2 tsp. ginger
1/4 cup melted butter

16 peach slices
2 tbsp. sugar
2 large eggs
1 cup corn flakes (crumbs)
1/2 cup milk

Stuffing: Combine cheeses and sour cream; stir in apricot marmalade. Place two tbsp. of stuffing into butterflied bread.

Batter: Combine eggs and milk.

Dip bread into mix, then dredge in cereal. Melt butter in large skillet and add bread slices. Brown on all sides. Then bake at 400° for 15 minutes. Combine both sugar and ginger (approx. 1/4 cup) in skillet; add peaches and cook for 3 minutes, stirring gently. Arrange on toast. Sprinkle with powdered sugar. Serve with warm maple syrup.

Yield: 8 slices

Really Quick Banana Bread
(Mariposa Ranch Bed & Breakfast/Brenham)

3 very ripe bananas	1/4 cup butter, melted
3/4 cup sugar	1 tsp. baking soda
Pinch of salt	1 tbsp. water
1 egg, beaten	2 cups flour

Mash bananas with a fork. Blend in sugar, salt, and beaten egg. Stir in melted butter. Dissolve soda in water and add to mixture. Blend in flour. Pour into greased and floured 9" x 5" x 3" loaf pan. Bake at 350° for 1 hour. Cool partially before removing from pan.

Cook's Note: Think this is too easy to be good? Just try it!

Yield: 1 small loaf of bread

Duke's Migas *or* Fairview Olé
(Fairview - A Bed & Breakfast Establishment/Austin)

8 eggs	1 cup broken tortilla chips
1/4 cup cream, or Half & Half	1/2 cup Cheddar cheese, grated
2 tbsp. butter, divided	4 tbsp. spicy salsa
3 tbsp. mild salsa	*Garnish: tortilla chips and fresh parsley*

Combine eggs, 1 tablespoon butter and cream in mixing bowl. Beat with a wire whisk. Melt 1 tablespoon butter in heavy skillet. Add egg mixture and stir in mild salsa. Scramble eggs until they begin to set. Add broken tortilla chips, stirring to mix. Divide egg mixture, placing 1/4 on individual plates. Top each with grated cheese and 1 tablespoon of spicy salsa. Garnish with tortilla chips and a sprig of fresh parsley. Enjoy!

Serves: 4

Index of HAT Properties

1890 House Bed & Breakfast Inn (The) 28

A Yellow Rose Bed & Breakfast 79

Academy House of Monte Vista 78

Angel Arbor Bed & Breakfast Inn 55

Angelsgate Bed & Breakfast 21

Ant Street Inn 18

Austin Street Retreat 33

Bailey House 15

Bed & Breakfast on the Bay 59

Bolin's Prairie House 10

BonnyNook Inn 95

Brackenridge House "a bed & breakfast inn" 80

Captain Shepard's Inn 61

Captain's House on the Lake (The) 50

Carson House Inn and Grille 72

Castle Inn (The) 66

Chaska House (The) 96

Cleburne's 1896 Railroad House B&B 22

Columns on Alamo (The) 81

Country Cottage Inn 34

Countryside Inn 63

Crystal River Inn 85

Das College Haus 35

Das Garten Haus 36

Delforge Place (The) 37

Fairmount Hotel (The) 82

Fairview - A Bed & Breakfast Establishment 11

Far View - A Bed & Breakfast Inn 19

Gage Hotel (The) 62

Governors' Inn (The) 12

Gruene Country Homestead Inn 53

Gruene Mansion Inn 54

Guadalupe River Ranch 16

Harrison Bed & Breakfast (The) 97

Heart of My Heart Ranch 74

Heather's Glen... A Bed & Breakfast and More! 25

Historic Kuebler-Waldrip Haus and Danville School 67

Hoopes' House 73

Hotel Limpia (The) 30

Hôtel St. Germain 27

Houston House Bed & Breakfast (The) 48

Inn at Salado 77

Inn on the River 47

Iron Horse Inn (The) 51

Karbach Haus Bed & Breakfast Home 68

Katy House (The) 88

La Mansion Del Rio 1887 29

Luckenbach Inn (The) 60

Magnolia House 38

Magnolia Oaks Bed & Breakfast 23

Mariposa Ranch 20

McCallum House (The) 13

McLachan Farm Bed & Breakfast 89

Metzger Sunday House 39

Miss Molly's Hotel 31

Moonlight Bay B&B 71

Munzesheimer Manor 64

Noble Inns 83

Noble Manor 65

Old Hunter Road Stagecoach Inn B&B (The) 69

Orchard Inn (The) 40

Oxford House (The) 90

Pearl Street Inn Bed & Breakfast 52

Pelican House (The) 86

Pride House 57

Prince Solms Inn 70

Rose Mansion (The) 76

Rosemary Mansion on Main Street (The) 98

Rosevine Inn Bed & Breakfast 91

Royal Swan (The) 84

Schandua Suite (The) 41

Schildknecht-Weidenfeller House 42

Schmidt Barn 43

Seasons Bed & Breakfast Inn (The) 92

Settlement at Round Top (The) 75

Settlers Crossing 44

St. James Inn 49

Terry-McKinnon House (The) 58

Texas Stagecoach Inn 94

Texas White House (The) 32

The Meyer B&B on Cypress Creek 24

Thee Hubbell House 99

Warfield House 26

Watkins Hill 45

Weinert House Bed & Breakfast 87

Whistler Bed & Breakfast (The) 56

Woldert-Spence Manor (The) 93

Woodburn House 14

Ye Kendall Inn 17

Yellow House (The) 46

Travel Log

Travel Notes